Praise for
truth. courage. *love.*

Many memoirs by successful women only tell the stories of a forward journey. In *Truth. Courage. Love.*, Terry provides a window into real life experiences and the emotions that goes along with life. The heartache of making difficult decisions, the glee of finding your person and place, and calm of living the full "width" and length of life.

> Kate Isler, Co-Founder/CEO of TheWMarketplace, author of *Breaking Borders a Remarkable Story of Adventure, Family and Career Success that Defied all Expectations*

Yet again, Terry Sidford shows us how to successfully live an authentic life. Her story has motivated me to step into my own best self, and provides the inspiration we all need to start our own journeys toward truth, courage, and love.

> Trish Walker, author of *Oh, Honey, I'm Just Getting Started, Consciously Create Your Next Decade*

My heart opened while reading Terry's down-to-earth prose. I felt myself rooting for her as the heroine in her compelling and unique true story, while simultaneously relating and seeing my own possibilities. I was profoundly inspired.

> Jill Orschel, documentary filmmaker

Terry Sidford writes a raw, and inspirational story about living an authentic life. She has taught me to Never Give Up and to find my Courage even when life seems impossible. This is a must-read book!

> Stacey Clavier, former journalist in radio and TV news

truth.
courage.
love.

truth.
courage.
love.

TERRY SIDFORD

Surrogate Press®

Copyright © 2022 Terry Sidford
All rights reserved.

No part of this publication may be reproduced, stored in a retrieval system, or transmitted in any form or by any means, electronic, mechanical, photocopying, recording, or otherwise, without written permission of the author.

Published in the United States by
Surrogate Press®
an imprint of Faceted Press®
Surrogate Press, LLC
Park City, Utah
SurrogatePress.com

ISBN: 978-1-947459-72-4
Library of Congress Control Number: 2022921780

Book cover design by: Michelle Rayner, Cosmic Design
Interior design by: Katie Mullaly, Surrogate Press®

This book is dedicated to my loving family, friends, and people I've encountered along my life's journey.

I would not be where I am today without you.

Table of Contents

PART ONE
Chapter 1: Before the Storm 3

Chapter 2: Where Did My Mother Go? 9

Chapter 3: Divorce, American Style 18

PART TWO
Chapter 4: A Difficult Transition 37

Chapter 5: Learning to Trust by Trial and Error 46

Chapter 6: Finding Forgiveness 58

Chapter 7: Settling for Stability 65

PART THREE
Chapter 8: The Courage to Be Me 87

Chapter 9: Stepping into My Authentic Self 94

Chapter 10: Today 104

Chapter 11: Afterthoughts 112

Acknowledgments 119

About the Author 121

PART ONE

Truth

Before the Storm
Chapter ONE

Encinitas, California, was an idyllic place to grow up in the '60s and '70s. About one hundred miles south of Los Angeles, Encinitas was a little-known beach community back then of surfers, flower farmers, hippies, and visiting celebrities who wanted to get away from the watchful eye of Hollywood. The Encinitas beaches of fifty years ago were uncrowded and pristine, and to have a home with a pool, up on a hill overlooking the ocean, was a luxury that just about any middle-class family could afford back then.

A middle-class family just like mine, for example.

Up through about the age of five, I lived with my average, mid-twentieth century family in Encinitas, up on a hill, in a big house with a pool. Our family consisted of two parents and three kids—like just about everyone else's. There was my big sister Debi (five years older than me), my big brother Dan (three years older than me), and the baby (me). And even though my now-grown siblings might not remember it exactly the same as how I remember it, back then I felt like we were the epitome of a happy family, straight out of a 1960s sitcom like *Leave it to Beaver* (if you don't know that show, feel free to Google it).

For the most part, I was a curious, noisy little girl, always wanting to be involved with whatever my older sister was doing, much to her annoyance. She was so cool, and I wanted to be just like her. Back then, Debi was into the '70s clothing styles big time, which totally impressed me. She wore things like a leather-fringed vest, hip leather hats, and dramatic lipstick and makeup. She

truth. courage. love.

had magical posters on the walls in her room that lit up with fluorescent lights, and she did trendy, artful things like paint beach rocks and make candles. Even though Debi objected, I somehow convinced my mom that I should always be allowed to join in when Debi had sleepovers, so Mom told her to let me sleep in the same room as her and her friends on those nights. My poor sister was not happy about this, and I knew it, but I didn't care.

Even though she was only five years older than me, I looked up to Debi like she was another adult in the family. In fact, later on in life, she dutifully stepped in and filled the role as a mom for me (which I greatly appreciated then and now). It was easy back then to rely on her because she simply took charge when needed, especially in a crisis or an emergency, and eventually there were plenty of both. She could assess a situation and then instantly know what to do. And since she was the eldest, I dutifully obeyed when she laid out a plan.

My brother and I, on the other hand, fought all the time since we were closer in age. This dynamic, however, only lasted for the duration of our childhood. We grew up to become very close as adults. Unlike Debi, who was always looking out after me, Dan was always busy making (or tearing apart and rebuilding) something. I will never forget the time he converted my playhouse into a bike shop, without asking anyone, of course. That really made me upset! I went to play in my playhouse one day, and instead of my dolls and tea set, all I found were his dirty tools and bike pieces. I was not too happy about this at all…until he made me a bike out of spare parts for my birthday. But even then, I missed my playhouse.

Regardless of our sibling struggles, when Christmases rolled around, we kids became a united front. Every Christmas Eve, all three of us would sleep together in my sister's bedroom in the basement. One Christmas, when I was five years old, I awoke to my brother's tip-toeing footsteps above us. I was just waking up from the noise of the creaking floorboards, when suddenly, my brother came running downstairs exclaiming that he received a surfboard from

Before the Storm

Santa! When my sister and I ran upstairs to check it out, we saw that Santa left her a mustard yellow mushroom-shaped lamp, and I got a new bike! (A *real* one this time.) It was the best Christmas I could remember. It stands out for me because in my mind, we were all together as a truly happy family. I saw my parents as fun and loving to all three of us, and more importantly, to each other. I remember around this time getting loving, tight hugs, every day from both of them.

My mom was a typical, stay-at-home mom just like Carol on the '70s TV show *The Brady Bunch* (again, Google it), or so I thought at the time. She opted not to get a career-type job, but instead she stayed home and took care of her three kids full-time. She did all the typical "motherly" stuff that moms did in those days, like clean house, buy groceries, and make yummy tuna and pickle sandwiches with Fritos corn chips for my friends and me. When I started kindergarten, I rode the bus to school, and Mom was always waiting for me after school when I came home. She even helped me learn how to read and write. At first, I was slower than the other children in my class, so Mom spent time with me after school getting up to speed. But regardless of how much of her day she spent helping out with homework or shuttling my siblings and me around, she always allowed time to make beautiful meals. Every evening we all sat down to a home-cooked dinner, as if we were posing for a Normal Rockwell painting. After dinner, she'd sometimes sneak us dessert, which was a special, secret treat between Mom and us kids. My dad was into healthy eating and didn't want us eating what he considered to be junk food.

My dad was a teacher and went to school part-time to get his master's degree in counseling. But in spite of his career aspirations, he was very involved in our lives and always attended all of our school performances and events. He also made sure he was home for dinner almost every night, which was both a blessing and a curse for my mom. He was picky about what he ate, and that put a strain on my mom when preparing meals, even though the rest of us thought her meals were delicious.

My dad was raised by Mormon parents who owned and operated a health food store, long before healthy eating was trendy. Mom never really bought into the health-food lifestyle as extremely as Dad, and in fact, she thought a treat for the kids once in a while had its own benefits. Case in point, occasionally she'd whisper to us, "If you kids eat all your dinner tonight, I'll take you to 7-11 later and let you pick out a treat, like chocolate milk, ice cream, or candy. *But don't tell your dad.*" At the time, we thought this was something special with my mom, but in reality, it was part of a growing wedge between my parents. My dad did not want us to eat processed sugar under any circumstances, and even now, I have to admit he might have been a little too intense about it back then. My mom knew his feelings about sugar, and yet sometimes she'd let us have it anyway. Once in a while, my dad would find out about this breach of trust, and then my parents would have a fight about it. I never considered these fights to be a foreshadowing of *bad things to come*, but when I look back on it now, I see the writing on the wall.

The thing I appreciate most about my dad was that he loved having family outdoor adventures, and he made sure we grew up to value things like hiking and camping (which I do to this day). Most weekends we went to Moonlight Beach and had hibachi grill cookouts, played deck tennis, and swam in the ocean. Even though he could be very opinionated (especially when it came to food), my dad had a silly side that surfaced in good times or bad. But either way, it always still seemed appropriate and fun. For example, Dad was a master at hiding Easter eggs, which is probably why Easter is one of my favorite holidays, even today. I remember once he hid an egg on a life vest and then floated it out into the middle of the pool. We all saw it, but it was my brother who snatched it. He didn't hesitate to jump into the water to retrieve the egg.

Before the Storm

Another time, when we were visiting my grandparents in Utah, my dad took us to the Great Salt Lake. As the name implies, the water in that lake is very salty. So when Debi got salt in her eye, it stung and she cried. To comfort her, Dad simply said, "Debi, stick your finger in the salt water, and then stick it in your other eye. Then they'll be the same." I don't know why, but we thought that was the funniest thing ever, and we all laughed hysterically, which totally defused Debi's momentary crisis.

In addition to those outdoor adventures, I also loved playing with my friends Virginia and Lisa on the weekends that we didn't go to the beach. We'd spend hours in our own little made-up world. One of our favorite silly scenarios was pretending we were married to Elvis Presley or Davy Jones from The Monkees. We imagined our glamorous lives with them and played out whatever crazy, little-girl fantasy stories we concocted. When we weren't living life in our make-believe world, Virginia, Lisa, and I had a lot of fun swimming in our pool. I had a tea set that we would use to have a tea party together at the bottom of the pool. When we came up for air, we couldn't wait to get out and have a homemade lunch—courtesy of my mom and her famous tuna and pickle sandwiches.

But the summers were even more fun than daily life during the school year. Most summers, until I was in junior high, my sister, brother, and I would visit our grandparents (my dad's parents) in Orem, Utah, usually without our parents. We couldn't wait to get there! My grandmother, Emma, owned a health food store, which is how my father became such a health food fanatic. My grandfather, Harry, was a carpenter. My dad was just like Harry when it came to his silly sense of humor.

I remember on one of our trips to Utah, my mom bought us a big bag of some sort of gooey, minty, cheap candy that she encouraged us to secretly take with us and enjoy while we were staying with my grandparents. Mom specifically told us not to tell my dad or my grandmother about the candy. We didn't, and as a result, Debi and I quietly relished that candy all summer long behind my grandmother's back. Even though this sounds like a fun family secret, I have obsessed over my weight and what I eat, off and on, my entire life. I've always wondered if such obsessions might've had something to do with how our family was so divided about what to eat while I was growing up.

But regardless of these family dietary demands, those summer trips to see my grandparents in Utah were so much fun, and I still cherish those memories. Grandma Emma taught us how to cook and eat healthy, and Grandpa Harry taught us how to build things. They were fun, caring, and loving grandparents who let us do cool, grown-up things, like help out in the garden and work in the health food store. These were the moments when my siblings and I could be ourselves and completely feel free from any worries or judgment from our parents. Even though we were happy at home, we were *extremely* happy when we went to Orem for the summer.

For the first five to six years of my life, all was seemingly good and ordinary for me as a happy, imaginative kid. I woke up every morning eager to create something new and magical. I had great friends, loving parents, and caring siblings, and I saw life as fun, safe and exciting. Just as any kid should. My brother, sister, and I were happy—the kind of "happy" that kids take for granted. And it warmed my heart to know that my parents were happily married—or at least I thought they were. I felt confident that we were the typical, suburban, middle-class family and that life was good.

What could possibly go wrong?

Where Did My Mother Go?
Chapter TWO

Everyone has those pivotal moments in their lives when something unexpected happens, and then from that moment on, everything changes—forever. Sometimes the change is for the better, sometimes not. But either way, life is never the same. For me, that first monumental change in my life came when I was about five or six years old.

It started out like any other day. I went to school, did what I was told (because I was a "good kid" who was eager to please), and then came home without a care in the world. I went straight to my bedroom to change from my favorite plaid dress into my "play clothes," checked on my pet goldfish (they all looked fine), and plopped down on my bed to contemplate my next move. *Hmm. Should I round up my friends for an afternoon of make-believe? Or should I opt for swimming in the pool instead? Or maybe I could see what my sister was up to and tag along with her for a while.*

As I was daydreaming of all my options, I suddenly heard my mother's voice filter in from somewhere else in the house. Only it wasn't her normal voice. Instead, she was raging like I'd never heard before. "You don't understand!" she angrily yelled. "I hate you! Get out of here!"

My ears instantly perked up. My mother did not talk like this. This was not her. The intensity in her voice, as well as her brutal words, scared me. *Who could she possibly be yelling at?* I thought.

And then I got my answer.

"Laura, you need to calm down," I heard my dad say, also louder than normal. "Lower your voice. You don't know what you're saying."

I couldn't believe what I was hearing. My parents were out and out *fighting*. Not just disagreeing over some benign issue, like what to watch on TV, but verbally taking shots at each other like they were mortal enemies. I'd never heard either one of them utter a harsh word to anybody, let alone to each other. How could this be happening?

I held my breath and zeroed in on their conversation from my room. Quite remarkably I could hear everything, as if I suddenly gained superhuman hearing.

Mom was mumbling at times under her breath, but I could hear every word. "David, you think you're so good. But I can tell that you don't love me. I'm always here, taking care of the kids, while you're out doing whatever you want."

My dad returned fire saying, "Laura, you're damaging our family. Can't you see that? You need to get help."

"No, I don't," Mom replied, her voice dripping with irony. "*You're* the one that needs help. Why don't you just leave!"

My heart shattered into a million pieces. I loved my parents and our family. What does this all mean? I felt unstable, insecure, and confused about what would happen next. Was my dad going to leave us? How am I going to handle all of this? In that moment, my solid foundation crumbled out from under me, and everything I knew changed. All I wanted was to love and be loved by my family. In my little world, that was more than enough. I was so happy in our family life, but it felt like someone just took it all away from me in an instant.

Their vicious conversation left me in a state of confusion and fear. Even though nothing had physically changed—I was still in my room, in my house, with my family—everything had *emotionally* changed within those ten to fifteen minutes. I helplessly listened to what I realized later would become, for me, ground zero of the end of the family I had grown to love and depend on. After

Where Did My Mother Go?

I'd heard enough, I immediately I went to my friend Lisa's house to escape the painful emotions welling up within. While I was there, I didn't mention my parents' fight to her. Instead, I pretended everything was normal. It was my way of pushing down the ache in my heart that I didn't know how to deal with.

From that point on, my parents fought more often, more openly, and more intensely, until all concern for how they appeared in front of their children melted away. I realize now that they had most likely been arguing behind the scenes long before I noticed. But for me, that afternoon when I first heard them was the tipping point at which they couldn't keep their unhappiness under wraps any longer. I suspect my older siblings knew much sooner about our parents' discontent than I did, but since I was the baby of the family, I think everyone tried to keep anything unpleasant from me for as long as possible; a gesture that I understand (and even appreciate) looking back, but as a child, it made me feel, on some level, even worse when it became apparent.

My parents' visceral arguments continued almost daily. It got to the point at which they couldn't stand being in the same room together. I came to the conclusion that this was going to be our *new normal*, and I'd just have to adjust. My child-like hope convinced me that my parents would still be the same people they'd always been *to us kids*. It was only how they treated *each other* that would change. *I don't like that*, I thought at the time, *but I can live with it*.

But then something unexpected and scary happened. My mother's personality started to change. Instead of the caring provider she'd previously been, she morphed into this bitter, angry woman who sat alone at the kitchen table chain smoking and drinking something red at all hours of the day. She still went through the motions of being a mom, but it wasn't the same. Now she was like a zombie, and it all seemed to have something to do with *her drink*. One weekend, while my friends and I swam in our pool, my mother watched us from a lawn chair as she drank that red stuff *again*. I thought, *Hmm, her red drink must taste like Kool-Aid. And Kool-Aid is good, right?* When my mother left for a few minutes, I ran over and took a big swig of her "Kool-Aid." It tasted awful! I thought, *How could anyone drink something like that? Especially when it makes you so mean.*

But she kept drinking it. And the more she did, the more she withdrew and immersed herself in her own little world, during which it became difficult to get her attention. Even if you could get her to snap out of it for a moment, her lucidity didn't last long. I found myself frightened by this new version of my mom, especially when I'd catch her doing something strange, like mumbling terrible things about my dad under her breath to no one in particular.

In response to my mother's antics, my dad didn't do much better. Instead of self-sabotage, he simply dropped out. He spent less and less time at home, to the point that he sometimes didn't come home at all. Ironically, making himself scarce only fueled my mother's obtuse behavior. Their fights were replaced by her conjecture as to what he must be doing. The more he stayed away, the more Mom became suspicious of *where* he was spending his time. "I bet you Dad is having the time of his life," she'd say to us kids. "He doesn't care about us. He always gets what he wants. I don't care anymore."

Of course, when Dad did come around, the fights resumed, bigger and scarier than ever. When he left again, she drank even more. Although I loved my dad and missed seeing him at home, I became stressed when he showed up because I knew it would lead to a massive blow-up between my parents. This is why it was bittersweet when, after several months of this dysfunctional family torture, my dad finally, and officially, moved out—leaving us kids with an even more dysfunctional, depressed, alcoholic mother.

I was always the fixer and the peacemaker in my family. As a young girl, I thought I could fix any problem—a function, I'm sure, of my intense imagination. I believed in happy endings, and it was only a matter of how hard you tried in order to get one. When my dad moved out, I made feeble attempts at reaching out to my mom, but honestly, how much could a first grader do

Where Did My Mother Go?

to repair a marriage? I know now that their problems weren't my fault, but at the time, I wasn't so sure. I wanted to help, to be part of the solution, but any attempts I made to connect with my mom were weak and unhelpful. In response, she would simply brush me aside. It was her way of not involving me in something that would only harm me further, but to me it was pure rejection by someone I loved dearly. In an effort to protect myself, I internalized the breakup of my parents' marriage as a problem that *I had failed* to fix.

Not surprisingly, my mother's downward spiral filtered down to her children. As a result of my parents' fighting and break-up, I had intense nightmares and my self-esteem plummeted. Suddenly, I struggled in school more than I had before. To her credit, as out-of-it as my mother was from her constant drinking, she did try to keep up with tutoring me in reading and writing, which was something I needed even more once my family fell into disrepair. But the quality of her help diminished considerably, and I did not welcome it as much as I had before.

My life became a revolving door of anxiety. I went to bed and woke up in a complete state of stress. I started wetting the bed often. In the first grade (when all this started), I had a teacher whom I thought was very mean. I'm sure outside of the classroom she was a perfectly nice person, but at school she was different, and as a result, she scared me. I remember one morning in class I had to go to the bathroom, but I waited until the very last minute to raise my hand to ask the mean teacher if I could leave to use the restroom. Of course, she said I could go. But at that point, my bladder was ready to burst. I sprinted down the hallway and around the corner into the girls' bathroom. As (bad) luck would have it, the toilets had just been cleaned and the seats were all up. I was wearing a dress, but I had to go so badly that I didn't have time to put down the seat, lift my dress, or even take down my underwear. As a result, I plopped down and fell rear-end-first into the toilet bowl. I started to cry as I finally relieved myself, and then I struggled to get out of the toilet, drenched in pee-soaked water. I was so embarrassed that I walked straight to the principal's office and asked them to call my parents to take me home.

My dad came to get me. Because he was a counselor in the district, he knew the principal, and I could tell they were all sad about the circumstances and genuinely cared about what I was going through. But the attention in that moment was almost too much; more like pity than concern—as if the principal felt sorry for this poor little girl whose family was a wreck.

But to his credit, my dad was not that way. He was loving and kind when he drove me home. In fact, no one in my family made me feel bad about the incident. Even my mother talked to me about it afterward and told me that those types of accidents happen to other kids, too. When I went back to school, the *mean* teacher was all of a sudden very nice, and the next time I had to raise my hand to go the bathroom, she let me go immediately.

But regardless, the war between my parents continued. With no relief in sight, I eventually got sick from all the stress. For no apparent reason, I came down with what they diagnosed at the time as the Hong Kong flu, which kept me home for a month with my alcoholic mother. One day, while I was home *all day* with Mom, she became overwhelmed by an alcoholic fit and threw a coffee cup out the front window. I was so scared I ran to the phone, called my dad, and pleaded with him to come get me.

"I'm sorry, honey," he said unconvincingly, "the courts will not allow me to come pick you up."

What? I couldn't believe what I was hearing! I was devasted and confused, wondering why I had to stay with my mother and feel unsafe.

From that point on, I tried my hardest to get my mother to stop drinking and smoking. I even cut up her cigarettes and poured her gallon jug of red wine down the drain, thinking that would make a difference—that she'd see how desperate I was and surely stop. Instead, it made her as mad as I had ever seen

Where Did My Mother Go?

her. She chased me around the house, so I hid until she finally gave up, drank more, and passed out in a drunken stupor.

From an adult's perspective now, I see that my mom tried her best to deal with her pain while maintaining her status as a mom. She made her attempts, like when she tried to fix my hair or dress me so I looked nice for school every day. Plus, she tried to make dinner for us every night, even though she rarely ate. But all this was little compensation for having to give up the mom I knew before. As a result, I just didn't have it in me to cut her any slack. Unfortunately, I didn't appreciate her efforts at the time because I was stubborn and resentful of her drinking. Now that I look back on how I acted, I can honestly say that I feel grateful she at least tried to be a good mother, especially when I can now better understand what she was going through.

Because my mom was a full-time mother, she didn't work. And because my dad was a full-time school counselor, he couldn't afford to support two households. My siblings and I stayed with my mother in our beautiful house on the hill, which left my mother to struggle financially. To help make ends meet, my mom rented out Debi's downstairs bedroom to some hippies. That room was a perfect lock-out rental, because it had a its own separate entrance. I honestly can't remember where in the house Debi slept after that, but I know it wasn't with the hippies. And I'm sure she wasn't happy that she had to give up her room. Being the eldest child, she had always had her own room before my parents split.

Regardless, I thought the hippies were super fun, and I had them all sign my red autograph book. (I still have that autograph book today.) But it turns out that having them as tenants was a sketchy situation at best. We eventually learned they were growing marijuana in our yard and selling it out of the house. In fact, we found out later that the police had been casing our house on suspicion of drug dealing. My mother didn't have a clue that these drug deals were happening right under our noses, as she was drinking and doing what she could just to survive.

Try as she could to keep us in the only home I'd ever known, we eventually had to give up the beautiful house with a pool and move into a small, cramped apartment. I was seven or eight years old by then. Not long before we moved out, my mother met her future drunken boyfriend, Jerry. I'm not sure how they met, but they had a lot in common, as he was also an alcoholic. My siblings and I didn't like Jerry. He was mean when he drank, and Mom and Jerry drank together often. He even moved into the same apartment complex two doors down from us, just to be near my mom, which meant Jerry was around *all the time*. Suddenly, our life began to feel *even more* uncomfortable and unsafe.

I remember one night my dad came over to give my mother a child support check. As usual, Jerry and my mother were very drunk. For no reason, Jerry attacked my father and ripped his shirt off of him. I was mortified and so scared. My dad left immediately, and I wished I could've gone with him, but every time one of us kids would tell my dad that we wanted to come live with him, he'd tell us that we legally couldn't do it.

On another occasion, my mother's sister and her husband visited us from Utah. Because our apartment was so small, they stayed in a local hotel near us, but they planned to do things with us during the day. One evening during their visit, Jerry, my mother, Debi, and I went to dinner with my aunt and uncle. My brother, Danny, missed out (fortunately for him) on this prickly event because he happened to be at a Boys' Club meeting that night. During the course of dinner, Mom and Jerry got very drunk (big surprise). As a result, Jerry started to embarrass us by yelling at the waitress for some non-existent infraction on her part. It got so bad we had to leave. Mom drove Debi and me home in her old blue Chevy, while Jerry drove back in his own car. She was so drunk, she slurred her words and swerved all over the road. Debi and I sat in the back seat in case Mom happened to hit anything like a tree or another car. Which thankfully, she didn't

Where Did My Mother Go?

After a few minutes of this craziness, Debi had had enough. While we were swerving our way home, Debi drew a line in the sand between us kids and my mom. "That's it. We're done. If Jerry doesn't go, *we are leaving*!" she declared with all the authority a teenager could muster up.

My mother just laughed at her. "Well, Jerry *is not* leaving," she said with a drunken smirk on her face.

When we got home, Mom joined Jerry at his apartment for more binge drinking, leaving my sister and me alone at our place. Debi took me into my room and told me to grab whatever we could. "We are walking to Dad's house," she announced, tossing me an empty pillow case. "Put anything you want to take in this, and then let's go."

I started to pack some things into the pillow case, but I was so confused and scared. *What should I bring and what should I leave?* I thought. *If I leave some things, will I ever see them again?*

Debi loudly, but calmly said, "Hurry up!" She noticed my hesitation. "We need to be out of here before Mom comes back."

"What about my goldfish?" I asked with tears in my eyes.

"Leave them." she said with compassion. "They'll be fine."

Debi called my dad and told him, "Mom and Jerry are too much. The drinking is *too much*. Terry and I are leaving now to walk to our house. You can't stop us. Come pick us up, you'll find us on the road." She hung up without waiting for a response.

I was so scared, thinking we were doing something very bad, and I was worried if I'd ever see my goldfish again. Then, without telling my mom, we left her apartment and started walking in the direction of my dad's place without looking back. I was only eight years old and Debi was thirteen. When we left, Mom was still at Jerry's apartment. We had no idea how long it took her to realize we were gone.

After that, we never lived with my mother again.

Divorce, American Style
Chapter THREE

After Debi and I ran away from home, Dad finally realized that it wasn't safe for us to stay with my mom. Being that my brother, Danny, was at a Boys' Club meeting that fateful night, he wasn't around when the chaos hit the fan, so he missed out on the drama. By the time he returned home later that evening, he was surprised to learn that both his sisters had moved out. You would think he would've immediately joined us at my dad's, but he didn't. Danny was very loyal and felt sorry for my mom, and decided to stay with her, in hopes that he could somehow help my mom get better.

Danny's youthful optimism wasn't as crazy as it sounds. It's only fair to mention that before Debi and I left my mom and moved in with my dad, my mom did make an attempt at getting sober. Although it ended up being short-lived.

Immediately after we moved out of our big house and into that teeny apartment, my mom realized that she was in way over her head financially, emotionally, and energetically. As a result, she moved all three of us kids and herself in with her parents—a nice Mormon couple in Utah who had raised eight children. Mom confessed her alcohol addiction to my grandparents, and in return, they bought her a mobile home on their property for the four of us to live in. They were determined to help her get sober.

At first, it looked like moving to Utah was the answer, at least from my young point of view. My grandmother sewed me new dresses, plus they had a farm with animals and a garden to play in. But best of all, the daily fear of my mother going off the deep end diminished, because there were other responsible adults around to keep us safe. I even started second grade in Utah, and I looked at it as a fresh start.

Or so I thought. Although my grandparents' intentions for getting my mom sober were good, their methods were questionable. Later in life, my mom confessed to me that during that time, her father would go to the liquor store and buy her vodka in an attempt to ween my mom off alcohol slowly. They knew she was going to go through terrible alcohol withdrawal, and he was trying his best to help. In addition, her father told her that God loved her and that she was a good person. It meant everything to my mom to have her father's love and support to get healthy, especially since my grandparents didn't drink due to their religious beliefs.

For whatever reason, this attempt at my mother's healing did not take. Within six months, we moved back into that tiny apartment in Encinitas, and our rollercoaster life with an alcoholic parent resumed. To this day, I'm not sure what happened. Maybe my mom found my grandparents involvement to be too much to handle. Or maybe Jerry kept calling her, begging her to come home. Who knows? All I knew was that for six months, we kids got a glimpse of how much our mom actually cared for us.

Which is why, I suspect, Danny hung in there with my mom a little longer after Debi and I left. Debi and I had it with my mom's drinking and with Jerry in general, so we tried to never looked back once we were out of there. However, Danny had an innate allegiance to our mom to do what he could to make things right for her. I was too young (and too scared) at the time to exert my will, so I just did what Debi and my dad wanted me to do. But when Dad finally stepped up and intervened on behalf of his kids, Danny convinced my dad that he should stay with my mom rather than join us, and my dad didn't press the issue—even though he probably should have.

truth. courage. *love*.

At some point around this time, my parents finally, and officially, got a divorce. My dad lived in a bachelor pad in the same town, and although it was enough for him, it was tight and cramped when Debi and I moved in. I visited my mom when I could, but it was still touch and go with her alcoholic mood swings. I remember one time, I was at Mom's place, and I had my friend April over to play. Without warning, my mom got burning mad at April and me for something that made such little sense at the time, I can't even recall what it was. Mom was so mean that the situation felt dangerous. As a result, we ran from the house and stayed away the rest of the day. I was so scared that I didn't come home until after dark. My humiliation in front of April was a lot to endure. It was beyond embarrassing that my mom scared not only me, but my dear friend, as well.

After that, April and I became close friends, probably because we shared this bonding experience of being intimidated by my mom. We were in the same third grade class at school, and we had not one, but two teachers, Miss Green and Miss Campbell. Somehow, my teachers were told (probably by my dad) that if my mother showed up at school, not to let her pick me up. I'm pretty sure my teachers (as well as April's parents) felt sad for me, because one night, Miss Green and Miss Campbell invited April and me to join them for a spaghetti dinner. I will never forget how special that made me feel. I will forever be grateful to them for offering their kindness exactly when I needed it.

About six months after Debi and I moved in with my dad, Danny also left my mom and came to live with us at my dad's house. To his credit, Danny stayed as long as he could, because he wanted to protect her. But eventually, her addiction got so bad that *she told him* he needed to leave, too. I have no doubt now that it was her way of protecting my sweet, loving brother, but it must have been devasting for him to hear our mother tell him that she didn't want him to live with her anymore, especially after he had made the effort to protect her and be there for her. Even though he was too young to understand, my alcoholic, foggy-brained mother knew it just wasn't safe for him to continue to live with her.

Now all us kids were together again, which unfortunately left my mom alone with Jerry. Once it became apparent that the three of us were permanent fixtures in Dad's home, he did his best to provide for us while working full time. Eventually, he bought a house in Escondido, which is pretty far inland from the beach (and therefore, far from my mom). Debi, Dan, and I thought the new house was super cool. It had been a long time since we had lived in what we considered to be a "normal" home. Plus, we all had our own rooms again!

Although things were getting better at face value, during this time, I still had nightmares that were bad enough to wake me up in the middle of the night screaming. It took my family hours to calm me down. I realize now that this was the internal pain from not having my mother with me. It was ironic that I was fearful of my mother when I was with her, but I also had a lot of fear and anxiety when I was separated from her. At the time, my childhood brain could not reconcile how to handle this, and this was long before anyone thought to get kids into counseling.

By now, my older siblings were fully engulfed in their teenage years, which caused a lot of changes in and of itself. I was eleven years old, Danny was fourteen, and Debi was sixteen. Like every other teenage boy in the '70s, Danny grew his hair out long and listened to bands like the Doors, Credence Clearwater Revival, and Edgar Winter. And I loved his music! Debi was busy with school activities, particularly in music and theater, and I was into gymnastics. Dad was gone a lot, so he hired a lady to cook vegetarian dishes for us and clean the house. I remember consuming veggie sausages and protein drinks in the morning that tasted so nasty, I could hardly get them down. (The plant-based food of today has come a long way.) I loved school again, and after school, I loved the fact that I could have my friends over to do regular kid things like watch *I Dream of Jeannie* or *Gilligan's Island*. Additionally, I loved not having to worry about my mother coming out of nowhere to terrorize us. In our own way, we all kept busy, and at least for the time being, life felt happy again for the most part.

Dad also moved on with his life, much more seamlessly than Mom. Embracing the '70s, Dad also grew his hair out, wore pooka shells, and enjoyed the swinging single life to the fullest. He dated frequently and didn't lack in female companionship. Eventually, he settled on one woman, and that's when *Sally* (not her real name) moved in with us as Dad's live-in girlfriend. She was pretty and liked to do fun things with us. And truth be told, it felt nice to have a stable mother figure in the house.

It was still an adjustment to share a home with my dad's live-in girlfriend, though. Sometimes it could be strenuous, especially since we were all at challenging ages, even for a functional family. For example, Debi was a teenager and didn't need anyone telling her what to do. Dan was off in his own little world. And I, as the baby, needed reassurance that we had a stable home that didn't include a crazy, screaming adult.

To be fair, Sally didn't expect us to think of her as a mother, but more as a supportive friend. And because Sally was fit (she loved dancing and music), we enjoyed going on family outdoor adventures with her. She even let Dad take the lead in making most of the family decisions, which we felt good about, because then it seemed like we were a real family—not because she gave in to him, but because there wasn't the constant fighting and tension that existed before.

Nevertheless, that's not to say that things were perfect. How could they be when you decide to live with three children that aren't yours? Occasionally, we kids would do something that upset Sally, and when that happened, instead of just telling us what bothered her, she'd put her two cents in with my dad. Then Dad would have to give us the bad news that Sally was upset about something we did. This added a different undertone of family tension. However, it was nothing compared to the conflicts with my mother. But now that I look back, Sally was courageous to take on three children. She didn't have any children of her own, so parenting was not a skill she had developed by the time we came along. Honestly, she was very brave to jump into this "instant family" situation with my dad. Overall, Sally was an upbeat, happy addition to our household, but most importantly, she made my dad happy. And that made his kids' lives happy.

Mom, however, was more unhappy than ever now that all three of her children had moved out. But given her condition, there was no way the courts would let her have us back, and she knew it. So instead, she resorted to other (less legal) methods to try to see her daughters. I remember one time, right before we moved to the new house in Escondido, but before Danny came to live with us, my mother came over to my dad's house while Debi and I were home after school. Dad was still at work, so her plan was to physically take us from our father. How she planned to pull that off, since we were pretty big by then, I had no idea. As she yelled, in her drunken voice, from outside the house that we belonged to her, we hid in the bushes outside and watched her performance in stunned amazement.

Needless to say, we did not go with her. Eventually, she gave up and went home. It was shortly after that when my brother moved in with us at my dad's.

From then on, my mother focused her energy and attention on her alcoholic boyfriend, Jerry. Before (and after) we all moved out, Jerry came over to my mom's place all the time and drank with her. He was much older than Mom and scared us when he drank (he was a mean drunk), so we hated life when he was around—which was often. Since he lived just two doors down from my mom, he was a daily fixture in our lives pretty early on, and he continued to be even after we moved out. If we came over to see my mom, that meant we had to see Jerry as well, whether we liked it or not.

truth. courage. *love.*

We all hoped this thing with Jerry would run its course, but instead, my mom married him. Although life was more even-keeled at my dad's, I still missed my mother terribly and would try to call her often, but it was a double-edged sword. If I mustered up the courage to visit her, that meant I had to endure her *and Jerry*.

Then Mom became pregnant with Jerry's child shortly after they married. She was so surprised to get pregnant in her thirties, but she was also excited to have another child. Nine months later, she gave birth to my younger brother John, and I was excited not to be the youngest child anymore.

After Mom had John, she finally decided that she had to get her act together, and she officially started her recovery from her alcohol addiction. She went back to school to become a registered nurse and Jerry tried to stop drinking as well to support my mother and their baby. The two of them bought a house in Vista, California, and started to have a somewhat normal life (at least it was normal compared to what it had been).

But Jerry's health was deteriorating, accelerated by alcohol, I'm sure. After they moved to Vista, Jerry had several strokes and was told by doctors that he had to stop drinking. My mom was already working on her own sobriety, so she had no trouble supporting Jerry's efforts to give up drinking. And eventually, they both did—sort of.

Even though Mom was determined to get sober, she still struggled with sobriety, because she had a lot on her plate: going to school, working full time, and taking care of a child, as well as a sick husband who was clearly unhappy when he was off alcohol. Jerry didn't necessarily take his frustration out on my mom, but he did yell at my younger brother, John, constantly. Mom knew this wasn't healthy for Jerry or John, but at the time, she felt she had no choice but to try to make it work and do what she could to keep the peace. Sometimes the pressure was just too much, and she would take a drink just to get a break.

Divorce, American Style

Jerry was not much better. His health continued going downhill fast, with or without alcohol. After his strokes, he had to walk with a cane, and he became so debilitated that he could no longer work. To this day, I don't know the specifics of his declining condition. I just assumed his health troubles were all alcohol-related. Jerry stayed home and took care of my little brother while my mom worked, which I'm sure was completely emasculating for Jerry, causing him to relapse back to drinking. Sometimes during his tirades he'd hit John with his cane out of frustration, under the guise of "disciplining" him. It was an unfortunate and challenging time for John, and my heart went out to him.

Due to their occasional relapses, I was worried for my little brother. I would call every other day just to check in on him and make sure he was safe. By then, I was in high school, so if Jerry or my mother sounded drunk when I called, I would drive over to their place to make sure John was okay. He was young and very cute, and I worried like crazy about him. I made it my business to visit John often. As an unexpected bonus, because I came around more frequently, I began to have a somewhat civil relationship with my mom.

Then suddenly, but not really unexpectedly, Jerry passed away when John was in high school. In a sense, it was probably a relief for my mom, although I don't think she'd ever admit it; she loved Jerry and felt supported by him. After Jerry was gone, my mother had more success at getting sober. She also knew she had to take care of John by herself now. With Jerry's negative energy out of the house, John and my mom could lead more peaceful lives, and eventually, they became very close. That serenity also spilled over into other parts of her life. She got a great job at Tri-City Medical Center in Oceanside, made new friends, and started doing things with them. She even occasionally dated once in a while.

When John turned eighteen, he left home. After that, Mom sold her house in Vista and moved into an apartment by herself, where she appeared to be happier than she'd been in a long time. She eventually met and married a man named Robert Elsasser. It was her third time at the altar, and this time it worked. They were married for twenty-two years, and they had a fun, somewhat healthy relationship compared to her first two marriages. The best thing about Robert was that he was very supportive of her sobriety, making sure she never relapsed again. And as a result, she finally became completely, one hundred percent sober.

Later in life she'd have a glass of wine for a special event and then stop. She wouldn't have another drink until the next special occasion, which could be months or years away. Seeing her have that occasional drink at that stage in her life always made my siblings and me feel uneasy. But to her credit, she never let alcohol consume her or get the best of her again.

Terry Sidford

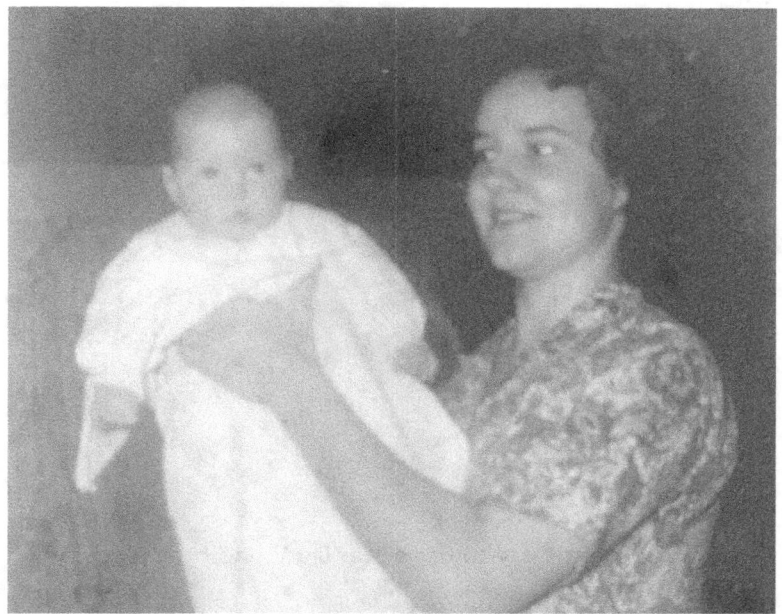

Terry at age two months with her mom.

Terry at age three in American Samoa with her parents, her sister Debi, and brother Danny.

truth. courage. *love*.

Terry at age three with her sister Debi and brother Danny.

Terry at age four with her sister Debi.

Terry Sidford

Terry at age five on Christmas with her mother, sister Debi and brother Danny.

Terry at age five with Debi and Danny at the Del Mar Fair.

truth. courage. *love.*

Terry at age five with Debi and Danny visiting grandparents in Orem, Utah.

Terry at age five with her sister Debi and brother Danny.

Terry Sidford

Terry at age five with Debi and Danny on Christmas morning in Encinitas, California.

Terry at age six. Bryce Canyon.

truth. courage. love.

Terry at age six dancing at school for Cinco de Mayo.

Terry at age six or seven in a school photo.

Terry Sidford

Terry at age seven or eight with her father.

Terry at age thirteen with brother Danny and her father on a summer trip to Northern California.

truth. courage. *love*.

Terry at age thirteen with brother Danny and her father on a summer trip to Northern California.

Terry at age thirteen playing tennis with her father.

PART TWO

Courage

A Difficult Transition
Chapter FOUR

While Mom sorted out her life with Jerry, my siblings and I finally had somewhat of a normal life living in Escondido with my dad and his live-in girlfriend, Sally. Although Sally was more of a friend than a parent, her occasional annoyance with us kids felt like a dream compared to the nightmare it had been living with my mom. Sally helped add more fun and happiness to our family life. With this new (and now consistent) status quo, I slowly began to regain my confidence both at school and at home.

But little did I know, I was about to endure a series of changes that would once again upset my already turbulent childhood. After Debi graduated from high school, she was off to college. Of course, being a kid, I just assumed she'd go to college somewhere nearby in California and live at home as she always had. Kids are not big on change, and I'd felt I'd certainly had enough of it in my life by that point. But Debi had bigger and better plans; she had been taking lessons from some missionaries, and to my surprise, Debi converted to be a Mormon. But in retrospect, it makes sense. Like the rest of us, Debi looked up to our grandmother, who was also Mormon, and since (like the rest of us) Debi was looking for stability in her life, converting to Mormonism gave her what she wanted. She moved to Utah to attend Brigham Young University.

She thrived during her time at BYU, both academically and socially. She even joined a musical group that traveled all over the country to perform. And as an added bonus, she started dating a young man in that group who went on to become a serious boyfriend. So serious, in fact, that after college, he became her first husband, and they moved to Arizona to start a family.

That left just Danny and me at home with my dad and Sally.

But not for long.

After Debi left, the house in Escondido seemed a little big, so Dad and Sally moved us to an apartment in Carlsbad, which was conveniently located across the street from the beach. By then, Danny was a sophomore in high school and I was in seventh grade.

Truth be told, I think part of the reason Dad and Sally moved back to the beach was because Sally previously had an apartment there, and they wanted to be a part of the "hip scene" that wasn't really available in the suburbs of east San Diego County. After we moved, Dad started taking EST self-improvement classes. EST stands for Erhard Seminars Training, and was founded in 1971 by Werner Hans Erhard, an American author and lecturer known for his brand of personal and professional development workshops. The whole idea behind EST was that (once you knew how) you could transform your life for the better, simply by leaning into and experiencing the process of life itself (easier said than done for most people). There were so many mixed opinions about EST at the time. Some loved it and found value in it, while others went so far as to call it a cult. Either way, within thirteen years it went under and eventually morphed into the Landmark Forum, which still exists today.

But back then my dad was in search of personal improvement, and EST resonated with him as a way to achieve it. He became such a believer in EST that he wanted to share it with the people he loved, including his kids. In all his enthusiasm, I remember one time, when I was eleven years old, Dad took Danny and me to learn a Transcendental Meditation practice. At the time, I thought it was just another one of Dad's crazy things he was into. But as it turns out, I'm so grateful that he introduced me to meditation at such a young age. I still use TM to mediate, and I now realize that Dad was on the cutting edge of self-improvement teachings.

A Difficult Transition

After that, Dad talked Danny into taking a teen ropes course in the mountains near San Francisco. I don't remember exactly how long Danny was gone, but I do remember that when he left for San Francisco, he had long hair and a hippy-dippy, teenage attitude, but when he came back, he had short hair and a mindset that he could do anything.

I thought my brother's transformation was very cool; I couldn't believe how much he'd changed just by taking a ropes course! So, when my dad suggested I attend a different four-day EST teen training in LA—by myself, even though I was only thirteen at the time—I agreed to do it.

On the day of the drop-off, Dad drove me up to L.A., and all I had with me was a small suitcase and a sleeping bag. I was a little worried about the sleeping bag part. "Dad, why do I need a sleeping bag if I they're going to put me in a room with a bed?" I legitimately asked.

"I wouldn't worry about it," he replied. "I have no doubt the trainers will take care of you just fine and make sure you have everything you need while you're there, including a place to sleep." He was confident that all would be good and that I shouldn't be concerned.

I, on the other hand, looked at him as if he were out of his mind.

Turns out I was right. This was NOTHING like the ropes course Danny had talked about. Instead, I was thrown in with 250 at-risk, messed-up teenagers whose only interest in team-building was banning together if, and only if, they decided to rob a liquor store. I was not happy about this at all. To make matters worse, part of the introduction process was that I had to walk up to a microphone and, in front of everyone, *ask for a place to stay*. As I stood at that mic and looked around the room at all the defiant kids that obviously had to be there as part of some sort of punishment, I was justifiably terrified. After I mumbled out my request for a place to sleep, a sweet, kind girl agreed to take me in as a roommate, and it ended up being the perfect place for me to stay.

Regardless, the next four days were pretty hard for me to get through. The trainers were very strict. I watched them berate defiant, out-of-control teenagers, calling all of us *EST-holes* at the beginning. Since I wasn't *a troubled teen* who needed to be coerced into a proper behavior, watching this kind of treatment of kids by adults horrified me. We couldn't even go to the restroom unless they approved it. Role-playing was also a big deal in this process, and in order to move to the next level of training, we had to act out scripts until it was clear that we understood the message of the lesson. I remember having to stand in line, onstage, waiting my turn to be publicly interviewed by a trainer. As the trainer went to each of us, they stared five inches away from our faces before they spoke harshly. If I even itched, laughed, smiled, or anything, the trainers would get all up in my face and demand to know what was behind the fidgeting (or whatever I was doing). It was teaching by way of intimidation, and I was not comfortable with that method of learning, to say the least.

Of course, I was a quick study and saw how it didn't go well for any of the other attendees who didn't toe the line. It was the most controlled by other people that I had ever been in my entire life. Contrary to what my dad probably thought it was when he signed me up, it was not a carefree, fun, summer camp experience. Honestly, it was more like boot camp, where they break you down so you can build yourself back up from scratch and know what you're capable of enduring.

They were hard lessons to learn, but I have to admit, the overall experience changed me for the better. By graduation (at the end of the four days), it blew my mind when I realized how far I'd come. For example, as a part of the graduation ceremony, one of the trainers gave me a small card and told to me to turn it over so I couldn't read it. Then he told me to visualize what was the on the card without looking at it. I held the card in my hands, closed my eyes, and went through one of the visualization meditation processes we had learned during our training. He told me he had written down some things on the card and wanted me to tell him what he wrote. I kept my eyes closed and trusted the process. I remember laughing as I recited what I saw; an old yellow VW van, records, and other various detailed items. When I opened my eyes, he

A Difficult Transition

told me to turn over the card and read it. Everything I had told him was on the card. I was completely overwhelmed knowing that we have this ability within ourselves if we apply it. Even though I didn't enjoy the entire training at the time, the meditation and visualization lessons from this camp experience are a couple of the things I've referred back to throughout my entire life.

After I got back from my EST training, I actually felt more confident about getting through tough situations, but I still struggled with my personal insecurities. Looking back, I think I missed having a positive older female role model, like a mom. Sally did her best to be a positive influence in my life, but I still missed my mother. Without even realizing I had that void in my life, I asked my dad if I could go live with my grandmother in Orem, Utah, to finish out my eighth-grade year of school. My dad could tell that I was grasping at anything to somehow find my way in life, so he let me go.

I remember how different it was living in Utah as a teenager. For one, there was no ocean, which is a huge cultural influence in Southern California. But there were a lot of gorgeous mountains in Utah, which had a different vibe of its own. The environment aside, the biggest difference was that the mindset in Utah was very conservative, and I didn't feel like my laid-back California lifestyle and upbringing were embraced by the community. At the time, it seemed to me that the people in my new neighborhood were very nice on the outside, but you could still feel their judgment on the inside if you were not of the common faith. This attitude was the complete opposite of who I was (and still am) as a person. Plus, it was confusing for me, because even though my grandparents were part of the Mormon culture, they were not exclusive or judgmental of others at all.

Luckily, my saving grace at the time was my new friend, Lisa. She was around my age and lived next door to my grandmother. She took me under her wing and introduced me around, which helped me expand my circle of friends.

Because I switched schools (and states) midyear, the curriculum was different, and I had some catching up to do. I struggled with some of my homework, but my sweet grandmother would stay up at night to help me figure it out and get it done. It was a wonderful experience to have a stable home with a caring female adult who sincerely wanted to help me. But even with all her compassion and genuine concern for my well-being and success, I still missed my home and friends in Carlsbad, as well as my brother Danny.

As much as I tried to fit in, I knew fairly early on that the culture and lifestyle in Utah just wasn't for me. After I finished the eighth grade in Orem, I moved back to Carlsbad to start my freshman year in high school that coming fall.

The summer I moved back, Dad, Danny, and I took a trip to Puerto Vallarta, Mexico that would influence my life in many ways. As usual, Dad decided to wing it on this trip, informing my brother and me that we would find a hotel (in Mexico) when we got there. This meant that we had no idea where we'd be spending our first night in Mexico when we left California. Can you imagine that? Traveling with two kids that way? This did not make me feel comfortable.

But just as it always did with my dad and his crazy schemes, everything turned out fine. We ended up staying at a boutique hotel up on a hill, owned by some retired Americans. The trip started out good, and the three of us actually had a great time—until I got sick from the food. Not wanting to be alone in a hotel room, I sat at the beach under a *palapa* while everyone else had fun. I was miserable. At one point, a drunk Mexican guy tried to hit on me, and it made me even more sick to my stomach.

The next day, we went to the famous beach at which Richard Burton and Ava Gardner filmed the 1964 feature film, *The Night of The Iguana*. It was a beautiful beach, but I was still recovering from Montezuma's Revenge, and thus still sitting under our *palapa* while Dad and Danny went off exploring, leaving me alone.

As if on cue, I had *another* Mexican guy approach me, but this time I was ready to tell him to get lost. However, this guy was young and handsome, and he spoke perfect English, all of which caught my attention. His name was

A Difficult Transition

Fernando, and it turns out he was there with his parents for spring break. He lived in Mexico City and went to American schools (in Mexico City), where he was studying premed. He told me that he had seen us arrive at the beach hours before and that he had wanted to talk to me then, but he had spent all this time trying to get the courage to approach me before his parents wanted to leave.

"Can I take you out on a date?" he asked respectfully.

"Sure!" I replied, genuinely interested. Suddenly, my stomach didn't feel so sick anymore. I gave him the phone number of where we were staying, and when he walked away, I secretly hoped that he would call.

When my dad and brother returned, I told them about this encounter. Dad was suspicious. After all, I was only fifteen and a half, and this guy was eighteen. But Dad said he'd consider letting me go *if* the guy called. Turns out Fernando did call. After that, Dad said he'd let me go *if* Fernando picked me up at our hotel and met my dad and brother. Of course, Fernando did everything Dad asked. We went on our date, and it was the best. After that, we were inseparable for the rest of the week.

Meeting Fernando will always be a special memory for me, because when he came along, it was a period in my life when I felt very unstable and unhappy, but Fernando made me feel like a queen. He was kind, loving, and romantic, and to him, I was the most amazing person in the world. I truly believed *that he believed* he was the luckiest person ever to have me in his life. He felt emotion deeply, and we would talk for hours about life and beautiful things in general. Not only was this the first time I was *in love*, but also the first time I *felt loved* by someone I wasn't related to. When we weren't together, I anxiously waited to hear from him.

On our second to last night, we stayed out dancing until after midnight. When it came time to take me home, he drove me back to our hotel in his parents' car and parked it at the bottom of some stairs to walk me up the hill to our place. Everything was perfect, until all of a sudden, we were surrounded by the Mexican police. They took us in and charged us with a fake circumstance just to get money from our parents, which apparently was *a thing* the local police did back then as a way exhort money from tourists.

It was terrifying. At the jail, Fernando was thrown into a courtyard while I was given a blanket and told to sit on cement bunkbeds. There was a drunk next to me snoring, and on my other side, I could hear another police officer and a girl giggling and playing around behind a curtain. As I sat there, wondering if I'd ever see my family again, I saw a huge rat run across the floor right in front of me. I was scared out of my mind.

Suddenly, the police captain, a smarmy guy named Captain Lewis, sat down beside me with his white patten leather shoes, gold chains, and sweaty shirt unbuttoned for the full macho effect. "Do you want to go home?" he asked in a predatory fashion.

"Yes," I replied timidly.

"Then your family needs to pay us," he informed me, and then walked away.

I didn't know what that meant or what was supposed to happen next. But once Captain Lewis was out of sight, I bravely snuck over to the courtyard where Fernando was being held to share this creepy news with him. However, the police intercepted me, and Fernando was terrified as he watched them drag me away.

They threw me into a car with Captain Lewis, who drove me to my hotel. But before we got there, Captain Lewis suddenly stopped the car and tried to pull me towards him. Luckily, I had my hand on the car door handle and opened it, but he immediately started to drive again before I could safely hop out. When we finally got to the hotel, Dad was supposed to have left me a key to unlock the gate so I could get in. It was the wee hours of the morning, but I guess Dad wasn't too concerned about his daughter being out unchaperoned all night in Mexico.

As I tried to figure out a way in, the police captain tried to impress me by playing like a child with his gun. He then tried to corner me and kiss me.

A Difficult Transition

I pretended to hear someone coming and frantically rang the bell they had hanging on the front gate. I had to do this more than once before the owners woke up and came downstairs to rescue me from the creepy captain. The hotel owners quickly went to fetch my dad, who then paid the police. Once they had their money, the crooked cops left. Finally, the nightmare was over.

Except for the fact that I didn't know how to get ahold of Fernando's parents to let them know that their son was in danger.

However, it turns out that Fernando's parents were smart enough to know something was wrong when he didn't come home. When they called the police, they were told that the police had their son and that if they wanted him back, they had to pay the same type of ransom to get him back. Of course, they did and Fernando was returned safely. Later that day, Fernando showed up on our hotel steps to apologize to my dad.

After our vacation was over, I went back to Carlsbad with my dad and brother, and Fernando went back to Mexico City with his parents. But that wasn't the end of our relationship. We kept in touch, and he wrote to me with such deep and meaningful words that I would read them over and over again. Even though we had distance between us, our feelings for each other didn't die. Holding his love in my heart helped make all my worries go away, at least temporarily. I had never felt this way before.

And I liked it.

Learning to Trust by Trial and Error
Chapter FIVE

After we returned from our Mexico trip, I was due to start my sophomore year of high school, and Danny was going into his senior year. I was grateful that I'd get at least one more year at home with my brother, as I assumed that after he finished high school, he'd go off to college somewhere, just like my sister did.

But to my surprise, Danny didn't want to go back to high school. For whatever reason, he was in a hurry to get on with his life, and the only thing that stood in the way of that was his senior year. My dad didn't say or do anything to dissuade him, so Danny took his GED, passed, and then promptly moved to Utah to work in my grandmother's health food store. He also started selling a multi-level marketing protein drink, and in less than a year, he became the youngest person (at somewhere around the age of eighteen or nineteen) to make it to the top level of his branch. As a result, he enjoyed all kinds of "grown-up" perks, like being given a Lincoln Continental to drive around in for a year and attending top-producer sales retreats in which they'd fly him back and forth to the company headquarters in Florida via a private jet.

In less than a year, Danny was making so much money, he didn't know what to do with it. Did he miss high school? Not one bit.

However, I desperately missed my brother, because without him, that left me alone at home with my dad and Sally, both of whom worked and traveled a lot. As a teenager, I'm sure I was irritating (as most teens are), but because

Learning to Trust by Trial and Error

of their busy schedules, I felt out of place in my own home and felt more like a roommate. Without my siblings as a buffer between me and the adults in the family, I felt lonely and stuck, especially since my sister was just getting her life started with a man she loved, and now Danny was in Utah with my grandmother (whom I adored) making gobs of money.

Reluctantly, I headed into my sophomore year at Carlsbad High alone. My only saving grace was that I had a lot of friends, and those friends liked to party. Every weekend there was always a block party with a live band somewhere in the neighborhood. Although it was the '70s with the drug culture in full swing, I fortunately wasn't into the drug scene at all. But unfortunately, I did enjoy drinking a little too much.

Up until my sophomore year, the only times I had tasted alcohol was when I once snuck a sip of my mom's wine, and then much later in life, snuck a sip of my dad's whiskey. And I hated both! It burned my throat, and I thought I was going to die! But then, shortly into my sophomore year, I went to a wild party with live music and tons of people, most of whom were older than I was. While there, I drank beer and immediately got a buzz for the first time—which I liked. Then later, the mixed drinks came out, and I tried those, too. Before I knew it, I was legitimately drunk.

As I wandered from room to room, looking for Mindy (the girl I went to the party with), I saw things I'd never experienced before, like people smoking hash in groups and couples making out like crazy. I suddenly got scared and didn't feel safe. Eventually, I found Mindy, we got a ride back to my house, and then we crashed in my room with our bodies full of way too much alcohol.

Unfortunately, the party occurred on a week night, and the next morning, Mindy and I woke up to my dad yelling at us to get up for school. His voice sounded like a megaphone pounding in our heads, and the nausea was too much to handle. "No, we're sick," I groaned. "We can't go to school."

He knew we had been drinking, so he shoved apples and protein shakes in our faces, and said, "Get in the car now. I'm taking you both to school."

It took all the energy we could muster not to throw up in the car. After Dad dropped us off, we ended up ditching school and sitting under a tree most of the day until we felt better. This was my introduction to what it feels like to drink too much, but it wasn't enough for me to give up drinking.

Once Danny left, Sally and my dad traveled frequently, and sometimes they were gone for weeks at a time. I remember once they went to China for a whole month and left me home alone to fend for myself. It was lonely (and even a little bit scary) to be alone at that age around the clock, so I had my high school friend Stacey come stay with me whenever she could.

It was nice to have Stacey as company, but during Dad and Sally's China trip, an infestation of rats decided to move in. I'm talking about literal rodents with long tails and sharp teeth, as opposed to the neighborhood "bad boys" looking for a good time. I didn't know what to do. What does a sixteen-year-old girl know about getting rid of rats? The rats would eat any food left on the kitchen counters, and then stay up all night making loud scratching noises in the walls. It was like living in a horror movie.

To help "protect us" from the rats, Stacey and I had our boyfriends come over and set traps. God help us if we actually caught a rat, because we wouldn't have had any idea what to do with it, dead or alive. As we looked for strategic places to set the traps, we found my dad's stash of pot and rolling papers. We had never smoked pot before, but that didn't stop us from rolling a joint the size of a Cuban cigar. Clearly, we had no idea what we were doing, but none of us would admit it. (Who wants to appear clueless at sixteen?) When we tried to smoke the fat loaf of weed, it was so overpowering, skunky, and awful that after a couple tokes, we gave up. (I'm sure my dad would've been devastated over such a complete waste of his weed.)

Learning to Trust by Trial and Error

Not surprisingly, my self-esteem during this time was extremely low, and once again, I struggled in school; I had minimum supervision or guidance at home, not that I really needed it. Dad and Sally traveled and worked full-time, and I was a good kid, so I stayed out of any kind of "big trouble" that involved things like the police or school expulsion. But still, I realize now that my dad's absence after my siblings were out of the house weighed heavily on me. As a result, I don't think I truly felt the security of a home that kids—teens especially—should be able to take for granted.

Regardless, I loved my dad, and I know he loved me, too. But even so, it was up to me to find purpose outside of the weekend block parties. Since school just wasn't cutting it for me, I decided to look for a job. My decision to find work was also reinforced by the fact that I wanted nice things that were beyond the budget my dad had set for his teenage daughter. When he was around, I had no qualms about asking him for things that I felt I needed; important things, like…designer jeans.

Me: "Dad, can I have some money to buy some Jordache jeans?"

Dad: "Don't you already have a pair of Jordache jeans?"

Me: "Yes. But a high school girl needs more than one pair of jeans. I can't go around wearing the same pair of jeans every day!"

Dad: "How much do Jordache jeans cost again?"

I told him.

Dad: "No."

Suddenly, earning my own money seemed like a pretty good idea.

I got my first job at a place called Shelly's Underground; a small boutique clothing store privately owned by a nice couple. Turns out I was good at sales, and I ended up being one of their top salespeople at the age of sixteen. But since I loved the clothes we sold, it was a challenge to take home a full paycheck.

truth. courage. *love.*

The storeowners treated me with great respect, and it wasn't long before I looked at the owners and staff as family. We were there for each other, so much so that when one of the other young sales ladies, who was in college and single, got pregnant, the owners allowed her to continue to work there, regardless of what she decided to do about her pregnancy. Ultimately, she decided not to terminate, but instead, she had the baby and gave it up for adoption. At the time, her choice was puzzling to me, because I couldn't imagine carrying a baby to full term and then letting it go to someone else. That was a sacrifice I just couldn't wrap my head around as a young teenager. But the gift of time, wisdom, and experience has made me see that a big decision like that is so personal that there is no right or wrong choice. There's only your own choice. Looking back, I now applaud her for determining what was best for her and the baby, regardless of what others might have thought.

Having my own hard-earned money and doing a job that I liked for people who appreciated me felt pretty good. Suddenly, my self-esteem inched up just a little, but the better I felt about myself at work, the less interested I was in school. I started to skip class, quickly followed by skipping school altogether. My home life didn't get much better, either. Now that I was earning my own money, my dad and Sally expected me to pay a portion of the phone bill…at age sixteen! I felt like their roommate, so I started to resent them even more and acted out by sneaking into their room to "borrow" some of Sally's jewelry to wear to school. (I have to admit, she had some pretty cool stuff!) Sally was no fool, she saw what was going on, but she didn't know how to handle my teenage antics. So instead of confronting me directly, she'd write me little notes—which I'd promptly ignore. As a result, she'd get my dad in the middle of it. He would talk to me on her behalf, telling me that I was making Sally feel bad and that he wanted me to stop. I'd agree to what he and Sally wanted, and then we would be finished talking. Dad thought that was the end of it, but then I'd do it again.

Learning to Trust by Trial and Error

As an adult looking back, I can't imagine the frustration Sally must've felt from this annoying teenager getting into her stuff without asking. Not to justify my behavior, but I was so insecure about how I looked back then, that I thought Sally's pretty things would make me more beautiful. When I wore her jewelry to school, I actually felt better about myself, ignoring the fact that I was wearing someone else's things without permission.

This weird cycle between my dad, Sally, and me got to be too much for all of us. I was so unhappy at home that after my sophomore year, I decided to leave Carlsbad and move in with my sister and her husband in Arizona. My sister had always represented stability and safety to me when I was little, so it made sense that she could do the same for me as a teen. From my perspective, it looked like Debi was building the stable family life I had always dreamed of, so of course when I had the opportunity to go live with her, I jumped on it.

In Arizona I got a job in a hosiery store, but I did not enroll in high school. My sister was busy taking care of her young children while her husband worked, so they weren't able to hang out with me like my friends had in California. And since I didn't know anyone else in Arizona, it didn't take long before I realized that I desperately missed my friends and the beach community of Carlsbad. Within six months, I moved BACK home with my dad and Sally, and I found myself in the same mess that I had left. Except this time, I was too embarrassed to show up at Carlsbad High half a year behind everyone else my age. I did not want to repeat a grade in high school, so I studied for my GED, passed it, and got a job as a medical assistant working for a chiropractor.

I found that I liked the healing aspect of chiropractic care, and I started taking a few community college classes in general education, thinking that maybe I could do something in the health and wellness field. But being young, with no occupational guidance, I had no idea how to handle my time management, nor was I prepared for the stress of juggling work and school. Even though I had moved back in with Dad and Sally, they tried to offer advice, but they weren't sure how to help, being that they were busy with their own lives. Once again, I was more like their roommate, and as such, I was expected to help out with household expenses—adding more financial stress.

At this point, I was so frustrated with my life, mainly due to feeling like I didn't fit in anywhere—not in high school, not in college, not in the working world, not even in my own home. With nowhere else to turn, I did what my two older siblings had done when they both reached this point in their lives. I moved back in with my grandmother in Orem, Utah.

Although I loved my grandmother dearly, not being of the local Mormon faith was still a problem, just like it had been before. Nothing on that front had changed. I was still a fish out of water in the general Orem community. I really, really tried this time to fit in, just short of converting (which I didn't want to do). I got a job and enrolled at the local community college, but no matter how much I tried, everyone still looked at me like a square peg trying to fit into a round hole. My sweet grandparents would have done anything to help me succeed (and they were BEYOND supportive at the time), but it soon became clear to me that I needed my independence before I could truly trust my own judgment. I needed to try making it on my own. At the time, I felt there were too many people trying to tell me what I should do in an effort to point me in the right direction. As a result, I decided that I had to figure out a path myself, and I needed to establish my own independence to do it.

I moved to Salt Lake City to be closer to my brother, rented a room in a house, and went to work at a chiropractor's office. I decided that I wanted to be a chiropractor or a physical therapist, and I was determined to figure out how to achieve my dream, so I enrolled in community college AGAIN. I found that I excelled in chemistry and biology but struggled in other subjects. I tried working full-time and going to school part-time for two years, but ultimately, the strain of juggling both was too much.

Learning to Trust by Trial and Error

I quit college, which was both a relief and a disappointment. Looking back, I wish I would've asked my dad to help pay for my college tuition. I think now that he probably would've come through for me. But at the time, I'd convinced myself that I didn't need to rely on my family to figure out how to make it on my own and finish college. At the very least, I wish I had looked into financial aid, scholarships, work study, or anything that could've lightened my financial load. But I didn't, because I had convinced myself that I was safer not to rely on anyone but myself.

From that point on, I moved around from roommate to roommate, but I always had a stable job that I enjoyed. Eventually, my brother and I moved into a house together, and I loved having him as a roommate. Outside of raising my own family years later, living with my brother was probably one of my most stable living situations I'd ever had, and I look back on those memories of our time together appreciatively. Living with him felt safe, and that was something I hadn't experienced since I was probably five years old.

During this time, I dated a lot, and I had the pleasure of spending time with a few good boyfriends—as well as the displeasure of enduring some not-so-good men who pretended to be good boyfriends. Like most young women of my generation, I was very naïve when it came to believing that there were men out there with bad intentions when it came to the women they dated. I truly believed that if a man was nice to me, it meant he liked me enough to never want to hurt me.

A huge reality check for me came one day when a tall, handsome chemical engineer walked into the chiropractic office in which I worked. He was a patient, but while he was waiting to see the doctor, it was clear he was trying to impress me—especially when he'd show up to his appointments with gifts and flowers. Eventually, he got up the nerve to ask me out on a date, and of course, I said yes.

truth. courage. *love.*

Initially, we had a great time whenever we went out, and I could tell I was falling for him. The clincher came when he quickly became the "solver" of all of my problems. For example, when I needed a new car, he put money down on a car in my name and co-signed a loan. If I needed credit on anything, he signed me up, linking our names together, as if we were married. Then we moved in together on a joint lease. I should've been suspicious, but instead, I was enraptured! Here was this gorgeous man making all these grown-up, real-life sacrifices for me.

Little did I know that these were the opening moves of a seasoned con artist.

By the time I had my suspicions, I realized that I had signed on so many accounts with him that I almost didn't have my own credit identity anymore. Finally, I decided to ask him how all these credit accounts were going to play out. "Why do we have so many?" I asked him. "And how were we going to pay them all off?"

Until then, I had never questioned his motives, and he obviously felt threated by my sudden initiative.

He responded by snatching the keys to our car from my hands and smacking me across the face. He hit me so hard I flew to the ground. I was completely stunned by his surprise attack. Here I thought we were going to have a mature conversation, but instead it turned into a brawl! He promptly left in our car, and I didn't try to stop him. Instead, I immediately called a girlfriend to come pick me up, as I didn't know where he went or when he'd be back, but I sure as hell knew I didn't want to be there when he returned. That hit to the face ended it for me, and I assumed that it ended things for him, too.

And apparently it did...but not before he took me for every penny I had.

He drained our joint bank account and walked away from all our joint credit accounts, including the car loan (even though he had the car) and the apartment lease, a leaving me on the hook for it all. By the time he was done

Learning to Trust by Trial and Error

with me, I had nothing left to my name. I had nowhere to go and ended up sleeping on my friend's sofa. My credit was ruined, and my self-esteem was, ONCE AGAIN, at an all-time low. I had no car, no home, no credit, no money, all because I had trusted a man whom I thought had loved me.

And as if that wasn't bad enough, I found out I was pregnant…with the con artist's baby. I was mortified at the thought of having this man's child. I knew I would be bound to his abusive ways for life. I was so scared and frustrated. How could I let this happen? I thought, *How could I be so stupid?*

At first, I shared only the news of my breakup with my dad, and he begged me to come home to California to regroup. I resisted, because I thought I had to take care of this myself. I told no one about the pregnancy, but it soon became quite apparent that I had a problem I could not handle alone. Finally, I flew home, and once I was there, I told my dad and Sally that I was pregnant. To their credit, they were not judgmental or angry. Instead, we talked as a loving family, weighing all the pros and cons of all the choices available to me. And I will forever be grateful that I had choices at that time. After much discussion, as heartbreaking as it was, we all agreed that an abortion would be the best thing under the circumstances.

Luckily, I was only a few weeks into the pregnancy. I remember how terrible I felt about being in this position. No matter what anyone says, this is not an easy decision. The day of my procedure, my dad and Sally went with me to the clinic. Although I was grateful that I didn't have to go through that day alone, I felt bad for my family that they had to be the ones to take me. But at the same time, I felt their unconditional love and support, and that meant the world to me. We told no one else in our family. It was just between us.

After that, my dad begged me to stay in California to start over, but I was so embarrassed that they knew my big secret that I just wanted to get away, so I refused their offer to help. I guess deep inside I felt like I didn't deserve their help. Instead, I borrowed $200 from my dad and an old Impala from my grandmother. Slowly but surely, I worked my way out of this dark place. Luckily, I still had my steady, stable job with the chiropractor. However, on the flip side, I had to file for bankruptcy to get out from under all the debt this guy left me with. All this, while dealing with the emotional fall-out of terminating a pregnancy.

But time is an ally when it comes to healing wounds, no matter how painful they may be.

Eventually, I was able to move off my friend's couch and rent a room in a house, but it had no furniture, so I slept on the floor. I paid back my dad, gave my grandmother's Impala back to her, and bought an old, used Toyota. That room and that Toyota were all I had, but they were mine, and only mine. I didn't share them with anyone else, and no one bought them for me.

One night shortly after I moved in, I sat on the beige shag carpet in the middle of my empty room and suddenly started to cry uncontrollably.

I don't know how or why it started, but once the tears came, the emotional floodgates opened. Every broken-hearted relationship I'd had (and there had been a lot by then) just came crashing down on me all at once; my alcoholic mother, my unconventional father, the crappy men I'd dated, and then this con artist jerk who bled me dry emotionally and financially, and to top it all off, put me in the position to make the most heart-wrenching choice of my young life.

The tears just kept coming. And coming. And coming.

And then just as suddenly as the overwhelming emotion started, it was over. As I stared at the walls in a trance, I unexpectedly came to terms with my situation. Yes, I'd trusted the wrong person. Yes, I'd hit rock bottom. Yes, someone took everything I had away from me, including my dignity. But then I thought to myself, I'm still here. And I'm still me. No one can ever take my soul. I realized that my soul was still intact, and that I knew who I was. I was still the same person, I was still Terry, but I was a new, improved, wiser, stronger version. That was so comforting to me.

Learning to Trust by Trial and Error

In fact, that was the comfort and security I needed to know that I would do my best to never let this happen to me again. Will I make mistakes in the future? Sure. But now I knew that deep down I had the courage to pull myself out of whatever mess I stepped in.

After that revelation, I slowly lifted myself up off the floor. And then, over the next year, I slowly lifted myself back to where I had been before I lost everything. Little by little, I cleaned up my credit score, saved money, and became more careful about the men I dated. Eventually, I rented a new apartment by myself, got new furniture, and got a new car. I was never so proud of myself as I was for not giving up or running home for everything little bump in the road that came my way. It was enough for me to know that my family was there if I needed them. And with that knowledge, for the first time in my life, I had the courage to believe that I was able to fix my own problems—even very serious ones brought on by someone as untrustworthy as a deranged con artist.

This experience was the first time I was able to recognize my own my strength. I realize now that my strength and courage had been within me all along, but I never acknowledged either one until that moment, when I literally picked myself up off the floor after that momentous cry.

If I could survive this experience, and my childhood, I thought at the time, I can handle anything else life throws at me.

Finding Forgiveness
Chapter SIX

At this point, I was in my early twenties, and I started to have some clarity. I ended an unhealthy, abusive relationship, dug my way out of a financial hole, and rebuilt my life from scratch. Things were looking up for me, and I was finally able to admit to myself that life was good.

So why did I still feel incomplete?

Even on good days, I still had this small, nagging feeling that something was not right. However, it was never in the forefront of my thinking. Instead, it was like an annoying little tune that constantly played in the small, dark corners of my mind. It made me feel like something was missing from my soul. I couldn't put my finger on it exactly, but it was present almost all the time. Unfortunately, the more I tried to focus on it, the more nebulous it became.

The only thing I knew for sure was that, deep down, I was terrified of being abandoned...*by anyone*. As I got older, the feeling got worse. I distinctly remember the day I couldn't go on pretending like everything was fine. That day, I woke up longing to connect with my mom, so I called her, hoping to see her for Thanksgiving. Instead of agreeing to get together, she made an excuse that she had to work on Thanksgiving, which was probably true, given that she did often work on holidays. After that, we made small talk for a bit and then hung up.

When I got off the phone, I felt worse than before I called her. I cried uncontrollably with deep despair. And for the very first time, I actually felt scared for myself. Usually, I successfully buried my feelings of unworthiness so deeply inside that I could easily ignore them for long periods of time. I would sweep my unhappiness under the rug, convincing myself that I'd recovered and that life was just fine. But not this time. This phone call with my mom really triggered me, and I finally admitted to myself that there was some sort of connection between my degrading self-doubt and my relationship with my mom.

I didn't know what to do. I didn't want to burden my friends or family with something I couldn't even define, so out of desperation, I quickly looked in the phonebook for counseling services. I had no idea what type of counseling would help, but I needed to do something. I finally (randomly) chose a counselor and made an appointment. On the day of our meeting, I spent a good hour trying to give the counselor as much info as possible in the hope that she might be able to give me any advice that would help me figure how to handle my despair.

After spilling my soul out to her, the counselor came to the conclusion that I had a learning disability.

What?!? How she connected the dots between me feeling incomplete with me having a learning disability, I'll never know. Needless to say, she was not the counselor for me. But the fact that I just wasted my time and energy on her made me feel like there was something wrong with me that even a professional couldn't help. Disheartened, I drove home from her office crying the whole way.

But once I sat with some of the things that came out when I spoke to the counselor, I suspected my issues had something to do with my mom's drinking. I had heard about an organization called Adult Children of Alcoholic Parents (ACAP), which was endorsed by Alcoholics Anonymous (AL-ANON). I looked into it and found that they had their own Twelve-Step Program for adults who had grown up with one or more parents who were alcoholics, so I decided to check it out.

truth. courage. *love.*

At first, I just sat and quietly observed their meetings, but over time, I became more participatory. Even though it's obvious to me now that my mother was an alcoholic throughout my childhood, it was hard for me then to admit that her drinking had any lasting effect on me. However, after attending several meetings, I was able to come face-to-face with the reality that my mother was, in fact, an alcoholic, and because of this, she was not present as a functioning mom for my siblings and me when we were growing up.

This realization was a gamechanger, because now I understood why I had that nagging feeling in the back of my mind, even if I still didn't know what to do with it. Anyone who endures the emotional rollercoaster of growing up with an alcoholic parent ends up dealing with the residual pain in their own way later on in life. For me, growing up from age eight on without a healthy, functioning mother in my life created missing pieces that held me back from feeling fulfilled and emotionally whole later on. No matter how successful I became as an adult, it was never enough; deep down I always still felt unworthy of my victories and accomplishments. However, my brain would try to smooth it over by convincing me that everything was fine and that I shouldn't worry, because I had *made it*.

But then that nagging, little feeling of unworthiness would creep back in and manifest itself in the strangest of ways. For example, I always wore my hair short in an almost unfeminine way. I had convinced myself that I didn't know how to do hair and makeup due to the fact that my mother never taught me how. For the same reason, I told myself that I didn't know how to dress to look pretty or how to cook a nice meal. As if I wasn't capable of figuring out how to do all those things myself! And although I had a lot of female friends, I wouldn't let myself get too close with any of them because I was afraid they would leave me at some point, in much the same way my mom was out of my life since the second grade.

ACAP helped me confront my fears about not having my mother (whom I loved dearly) in my life and made me realize that I could sort out my issues without her being present. But in order to do that, I needed specialized, one-on-one help. I decided to try counseling again, but this time I did my research until I found a good counselor that I really liked.

This time around, the counselor did not diagnose me with a learning disorder (which was no surprise to me). Instead, she listened intently as I told her that in spite of everything that had happened, I truly believed my mother was a good person when she wasn't drinking. I knew she loved me (and all of her kids), and I knew she needed help to overcome her dependence on alcohol, but for some reason, I just couldn't reconcile how a mom could love her kids yet be so judgmental and mean when she drank. Intellectually, I knew it was the booze, but my childhood was still so painful for me, and I just couldn't get around it.

As I spoke, I realized that it felt good to tell the counselor how I truly felt and why I suffered because of these feelings. She was very sympathetic and attentive to my story, and I was grateful that I had finally found someone that truly *heard me*.

By the end of our second visit, I was done spilling my story to her (for the time being, anyway). When I finally took a breath and stopped my monologue, we engaged in a brief conversation that ended up being a turning point that changed my life forever.

"Terry," she said as she leaned back in her chair, taking in everything I'd shared, "have you ever tried looking at this story from your mother's point of view?"

"What do you mean?" I asked.

"Well, you've said yourself, many times, that you knew your mom was a good person in her heart and that it was the alcohol that changed her. Don't you think she knew that, too?"

I sat with that for a second, because I really had to ponder her words. "Yes," I said slowly, "I supposed she was aware that drinking changed her in a way that did not make her happy. And she drank even more when she was unhappy."

"Have you ever considered that she might've been doing the best she could, given the circumstances of her addiction?"

"Um, no," I thoughtfully replied, "I guess I haven't."

"How do you think she felt when she lost custody of her children?"

I didn't say anything, because I didn't want to admit that she was probably devastated.

"How would you feel in those same circumstances?"

Suddenly I was crushed. It had never occurred to me that my mom had demons of her own to deal with and that alcohol was the only option she felt she had at the time.

"Do you think she was hurting, maybe even just as much as you were, after she couldn't live with her children anymore?" she asked quietly.

I sat there dumbfound, knowing in my heart that the counselor was one hundred percent correct. "Yes," I finally admitted. "Maybe even more."

In that moment, it felt like a light bulb inside of me turned on and I could see everything clearly for the very first time. I cried, but they were tears of tremendous relief. I had always believed in my mother, but I never understood the full picture that surrounded her behavior. I felt ashamed that I had judged her so harshly. I walked out the door that day knowing exactly what I needed to do.

Suddenly, I knew the truth about my relationship with my mom. It was not *her truth* or *my truth*, but *the truth*. And the truth is this: A relationship is a two-way street. Which meant that I had to take responsibility for my part in my relationship with my mom. I could only take care of my side of the street and hope that my efforts would somehow make a difference on the other side. I changed my story that day from being encumbered by an uncaring, mean, alcoholic mom to having a loving, kind, supportive mother. I looked at her in a whole new way, and as a result, I started calling her more, just to say hi, and not expecting anything in return. And I always, *always* made it clear to her when we spoke that I loved her unconditionally.

Finding Forgiveness

At first, she didn't respond any differently to my calls than she had in the past. She was distant but friendly, which was our normal pattern. I persisted, though, and whenever things started to feel uncomfortable, I didn't let it trigger me.

Over time, the ice that had built up around her heart melted, and correspondingly, she called me more often. When we spoke, we had deeper conversations than we'd ever had in the past. She told me things no one in the family ever knew because she had felt unsafe to say anything. She had gone through a lot of pain and tried to protect us from information that we weren't ready to hear at the time.

I learned that her relationship with my father started to crumble early on when they moved to California from Utah. She was a naïve, young mother who grew up sheltered in a protective, loving, Mormon family. But early in their marriage, my father started to question the Mormon church and went in a completely different direction to find himself. He started to embrace things that my mother was not comfortable with, including drinking. In an effort to be supportive, however, she finally gave in to my dad's new ways and found that she liked drinking and smoking *a little too much*. Unfortunately, she found solace and comfort in both as a means to escape the pain and confusion brought on by a husband who was changing in ways she didn't completely understand.

Getting to know my mom's story from her point of view made me see that she was, in fact, doing the best she could at the time just to survive. I now know in my heart that she never meant to hurt us. With this newfound insight, I went from being victimized by my childhood to being courageous because of my childhood. I had made it through some very difficult years with courage and resilience. I had actually found strength through my adversities, yet I hadn't allowed myself to recognize that.

Instead, I *chose* to be a victim of my childhood. But when that victimization became clear to me, I then *chose* to stop being a victim of it. I allowed myself to change the narrative. My new story says that I have a mother who loves me

truth. courage. *love.*

and whom I love and admire deeply. It takes tremendous courage to forgive and to turn pain into gratitude, especially when you feel justified in your anger.

The rewrite of my story helped me see myself as a strong and courageous woman who felt connected to her best self. As a result, the empty void inside me went away, and I felt whole for the very first time. My mother and I became closer than I ever dreamed possible. I knew I could call her for love and support and she would always be there for me. And she knew I was there for her.

After that, I started to feel more confident and less fearful of the unknown. There is nothing more fulfilling than to be able to feel the full extent of love within your heart without the restrictions brought on by fear. As an added bonus, my compassion for my mother and myself seeped out into my relationship with the world. When I saw my potential, suddenly I could also see the potential in others. I found it easier to lead with an open heart, which allowed me to receive love and see love more readily in others—even in people I didn't know or just met! All of this made it much easier to trust my intuition, my spirit, and my journey. And once I was able to do that, I knew my purpose in life was to help others do the same for themselves.

From the moment I let compassion into my heart and saw my childhood story from my mother's point of view, the switch flipped for me. After that, I strived to be a better person by being responsible for my own life and how I responded to it. I may not be able to control what happens to me, but I can definitely control how I handle whatever life throws at me.

My excuse for failure was suddenly gone. There was nothing holding me back from creating the life I wanted—the life of my dreams. For the first time ever, I was truly confident that I could thrive and succeed at anything I set my mind to.

And that felt great.

Settling for Stability
Chapter SEVEN

Believe it or not, Fernando and I stayed in touch for years by writing and engaging in the occasional long-distance phone call. While I was sorting out the drama in my life, he was going to school in Mexico to become a doctor. We both knew that the other was dating, but I couldn't help but feel sad and upset when I didn't hear from him over long stretches of time. When we did connect, however, it was as if no time had passed. I could tell that he was just as in love with me as he had always been. And I was also very much in love with him, so much so that I would fantasize about dropping everything in my life just to go to Mexico to be with him. I think this fantasy is what held me back from getting serious about any boyfriend I had in the first half of my twenties.

During one of those long stints of not hearing from Fernando, I met Mark. Mark had been married before and had two young children. But he also had a stable job, and most importantly, he was kind, and made me feel safe and secure. I was still living in Utah, and back then if you weren't married and thinking about having children by the time you graduated from college, the local culture considered you an old maid. But that kind of thinking was not for me. I loved my job working at an ophthalmology office. In fact, I was excelling so much, this *job* was evolving into a lucrative *career* that I loved and that could support me.

truth. courage. *love.*

Mark and I started dating, and I knew pretty early on that we were getting serious. However, I kept him at an emotional distance, because the possibility of a life with Fernando was always tucked away in the back of my mind.

Then when I least expected it, I received a letter from Fernando telling me that he took an internal medicine internship in Salt Lake City at the University of Utah Hospital. His placement was no coincidence. He wanted to see if our relationship could work, and finally took a big step in that direction. Instead of waiting for me to come to him, he was coming to me. On one hand, him moving to Utah was a dream come true! But on the other hand, I wasn't sure if I trusted him after not hearing from him for long periods of time, over and over again, even when I reached out to him first. I had lost count of how many times I had tried to move on with my life after he disappeared. But then without warning, he'd eventually resurface, out of the blue, and as a result, my heart would lapse right back into loving him, just as it had done before. My emotional rollercoaster with Fernando was turning out to be a painful cycle. And as a result, I wasn't sure if his coming to Salt Lake City wasn't just one more time around that emotional Ferris wheel. Was I on the path to a bright future or major letdown?

To answer that question, I tried to be practical in my thinking. I now had Mark, a nice, stable man who wanted to marry me. Mark was safe. He wasn't the kind of man that would disappear on me. I had to decide between Mark and Fernando, and it was one of the most difficult choices of my young life.

I decided I had to come clean to both of them. I told Mark about Fernando, and that he was moving to Salt Lake City because of me. And I told Fernando about Mark, letting him know that Mark and I were in a serious relationship, and that Mark wanted to marry me. Both men were surprised and neither liked that there was someone else in my life.

When Fernando arrived in Salt Lake City, I picked him up at the airport, he was excited to see me, but also very upset with me, because I was seriously

Settling for Stability

considering marrying another man. I suppose he was justified in that he had taken a job halfway around the world just to be with me. But in fairness, he made his decision without checking with me first. He assumed that our love for each other would always stay strong, regardless of if we ever got together. But now with Mark in the picture, things were not so cut and dry.

Fernando was also good friends with my brother. Dan and I were roommates then, and we told Fernando that he could stay at our house until he found a permanent place to live. Understandably, Mark was not thrilled with this plan, but truthfully, nothing could have changed my mind. Fernando was like family to Dan and me. I knew it was risky to have him so close, but it was also a way for me to gage how much Mark trusted me and the foundation of our relationship. If he was sure that I would ultimately choose him over Fernando (even if Fernando was staying with me), then I needed to see that confidence.

Plus, I needed to see Fernando for who he was *now*. Were we still compatible? I really didn't know at that point. But if he wasn't what I needed, then I wanted to be able to end our relationship with dignity, once and for all, so that I could finally close that chapter of my life.

Regardless of my reasons, I found that it was much more emotionally challenging to have Fernando under the same roof. In order to keep it platonic, I had to keep my wits about me. I knew I'd made bad decisions about men in the past, and I didn't want to repeat the same mistakes. This time I was being cautious, trying to focus more on my desire to have a happy, stable future with a family. And I wanted to make sure that I chose a man that could provide all that for me.

Although I thought I was being very wise and thoughtful about the whole thing, temporarily living with Fernando in this way was incredibly painful for me. Clearly, I was still in love with him. But after spending time with Fernando, I knew, in my heart, that I should choose the security and stability of Mark. If I married Fernando, I knew that I would eventually have to live in Mexico, and that my life would be all about Fernando and that my wants and needs would take a backseat to his career. Plus, he had disappointed me so many times in the past by building up my hopes that we'd be together, and then letting me down with his long periods of absence. I really, really wanted to make the "romantic, fairy tale" choice and pick my childhood love, but I just couldn't risk being alone in a foreign country, with no employment possibilities, if things did not work out between Fernando and me. And what if we had kids? And then split up? What then? There were just too many unknowns to bet on a man that had let me down so many times. I just couldn't do it.

However, Fernando hung in there, hoping to win me over. But eventually I had to tell him, that although I would always love him, we just couldn't be together. He was still in love with me, even after I turned him down, but he reluctantly respected my decision. After he finished his internship at the University of Utah Hospital, he went back to Mexico to start his career as a cardiologist in Puerto Vallarta. Shortly thereafter, he met a woman (she was a pediatrician), and they started dating. They eventually married and had two children. And as far as I know they are still married today.

Fernando and I kept our distance after that, not wanting to interfere in each other's relationships and families. Regardless, we have stayed in touch sporadically over the years, and will always hold each other as dear friends who care deeply about each other. That part of our relationship will never change.

After I closed out the chapter on Fernando, I felt like I could finally, once and for all, move on. Mark and I married in 1989 when I was twenty-six. Living in Utah, I thought twenty-six was *old*, and that I was running out of time to have children. Mark already owned a home, so we moved into his house and started maintaining a family life with his two children; Samantha, eight-years-old, and Chaz, who was eleven. They were adorable children, and I loved them very much. We had them over to our house a lot more than the average "every

Settling for Stability

other weekend" that most divorced dads had with their kids, but that was perfectly fine with me.

Mark's kids seemed to adjust to having me as their stepmom without much concern, but Mark's ex-wife was not too keen on the idea at first. She tried to interfere in our marriage in her own way, making it abundantly clear to me that she was married to him *first* and *for a long time*. I was young and wasn't prepared for this type of treatment, and definitely did NOT like this aspect of marrying a man who had been married before. Mark's ex-wife eventually got used to the idea that I was permanently in the picture, and finally (over time) backed off to let us live our lives as a happily married couple.

At first, Mark and I seemed super compatible. He and I liked to do a lot of the same things, we had the same hobbies, and similar interests. We both liked to camp, bike, and cook. Shortly after we married, we built a new home in Salt Lake City, and it provided a perfect start to our life together. And as luck would have it, I got pregnant a year into our marriage. I was so excited, because I always wanted to be a mother who created a life for her children that was very different from how I grew up. I was still working for an ophthalmology office, but I knew I could figure out a way to combine my career with motherhood. I had established myself quite well at my office, and I was certain they'd let me be flexible with my time.

But life doesn't always turn out as planned.

When I was three-and-a-half months pregnant, I enrolled in a professional development course in Hollywood, California. I felt fine when I left, but while I was there, I started to have some bleeding and I knew that this was not a good sign. I called my doctor, who instructed me to immediately go to a hospital. I wasn't in any pain, so I decided to just get there myself.

When I called the front desk of my hotel to get a cab to the nearest hospital, they asked why. When I told them, they explained that it was their policy to call the paramedics in situations like this. I felt ridiculous, since I was only spotting at this point, nothing crazy! But they insisted. Within minutes, the quintessential extremely good-looking, young, California paramedics rushed into my hotel room to *save* me. I was so embarrassed, because I honestly didn't feel like I needed saving. However, I was secretly delighted that they were so handsome.

"Guys, really, I'm okay. Look, I can stand up and everything. I just need to find a ride to the hospital."

"That's what we're here for. We'll take you," they insisted.

So off we go to St. Joseph's hospital emergency room in Burbank. I was there for hours, waiting to see a doctor and get an ultrasound. But after several tests, the doctor confirmed my worst fear. Unfortunately, the baby had died, most likely long before I got there. But here's the really strange part. St. Joseph's is a Catholic hospital, and they told me they couldn't do anything to take care of my miscarried baby because they were a religious hospital, and therefore didn't perform the D&C medical procedure (also known as an abortion) needed to treat a miscarriage.

What? I was stunned! This was a legitimate medical procedure that had to be done at some point. And here I was in a hospital, where they could do it, but wouldn't. So instead, I had to fly home, knowing the baby in me had ceased to thrive. In flight, I prayed nothing weird, like a spontaneous natural abortion, would happen while I was on the plane.

Once I was back in Utah, my doctor told me that most likely there was something wrong with the fetus from the beginning, which is why it just stopped growing. He told me to try to conceive again as soon as possible. We did try, and I did get pregnant again fairly quickly. As a result, nine months later I gave birth to my son, Alex, in April of 1991. He was the absolute joy of my life. I could not believe how wonderful being a mother to this sweet boy was. When he was about eighteen months old, I told Mark I wanted another child. Mark briefly listened, but wouldn't acknowledge my request. Truth be

Settling for Stability

told, my wanting to discuss having another baby was the turning point of when things started not going well in our marriage.

Mark already had two children, and now with Alex he had three. At the same time, Mark traveled a lot for his job in medical sales, so he was pretty tired when he was home. But he never shared that those were reasons not to have more children. I asked him on several occasions after Alex was born what he thought about having more kids, always explaining why it was important to me, but he never gave me a response. Instead, he'd just dismiss me, which felt very invalidating. Here I had spilled my soul out to this man, but got nothing in return. Not even an argument, which would've been at least an indication that he was somehow invested in a conversation that was extremely important to me.

Even though Mark was a kind and loving man who was devoted to his family, he wasn't always good at communication. And me being young and immature, I didn't always respond with adult, calm communication. I didn't know how to improve our situation, or even where (or who) to turn to get help to learn how to improve it. Consequently, I felt like a failure when we couldn't connect. I realized then and there, that I needed to have a partner I could talk to and share my voice with, as well as hear their voice and their desires in return.

After much persuading from me, however, Mark finally agreed to have another child. But it took a while. Four years after Alex was born, my redheaded, blue-eyed baby boy, Connor came to us in April of 1995. I had his name picked out before he was even born, and sure enough, it fit him perfectly.

Alex and Connor were completely different. Alex had dark hair and dark eyes, and he came out screaming. Connor entered the world quietly, without a word, and not wanting to open his eyes. I was so happy with these two, I couldn't believe it. Having them kept me busy and distracted from the fact that things weren't exactly how they should be in my marriage, and that my relationship with Mark was slowly deteriorating. I downplayed the growing lack of communication between Mark and me, but as a result I started to feel hollow, like I was slowly dying inside. My nature is to talk and share everything with the people I love, especially my soulmate. But I couldn't do this with Mark. I began to wonder if I even knew who he really was, and if he knew me. I found our marital situation so conflicting, because Mark was a good man and kind. He was a great father, and our boys loved him dearly. How could I possibly be so unhappy married to him?

To avoid answering that question, I buried myself in my work and the children. But things that need to be sorted out have a persistent way of coming to a head. Mark and I started to argue more often. I tried to hold back my frustrations, but they would build up inside me to the point of spontaneous explosion. I would try to explain to Mark how I felt, but he just didn't understand. He tried to make it better, but for me it seemed like he just couldn't relate to why I felt the way I did. I relied more on my friends for companionship, but ultimately, I decided I had to do something different to change our marriage for the better.

As a result, over four days I attended a series of four training sessions at a life coaching school in Denver. Little did I know that this would be the catalyst that changed my life, *yet again*. During the training, I learned more about myself than I did about being a coach. On the last training day, we each had to create a vision and purpose for our life. And by doing this, I learned who my authentic self was, and it was not the person I was back in Utah. The instructor had each of us step over an invisible line when we became one hundred percent committed to living our authentic selves in life. This exercise made me realize that I had not been true to myself in my marriage. As a result, I was scared out of my mind to step over that line and step into who I really was. In class, I was one of the last students to step over the line, because I knew what that meant. But when I finally did have the courage to step over, I felt free and

Settling for Stability

more liberated than ever. After that, I knew I would never go back to not being myself.

I came home from Denver and told Mark that I was not happy in our marriage. It was one of the hardest things for me to do, but again my newfound courage led the way. I suggested therapy, and he said, "NO." Now I really felt stuck. And of course, I was concerned about how I would support myself if we divorced, and more importantly, how it would impact our sons. I decided that I needed to lay some groundwork before I took any drastic steps.

I started my coaching business and at the same time, applied for a pharmaceutical job in the ophthalmology field. But once I was pretty far along in the application and interview process, I found out the job required a four-year college degree. I didn't have a degree, but I had more than enough experience and was recommended by our local representative. I was called in for an interview and felt I had the job until my interviewer discovered that I didn't have a college degree. He didn't care if it was in basket weaving, any degree would have worked. He was so disappointed that he couldn't hire me on the spot, but said he would go up the line to see if there was anything he could do to get me in.

I left the interview feeling dejected and completely convinced that the job possibility was over for me.

But the day before Christmas, I received a call from the interviewer. "What are you doing on January 5?" he asked.

"Nothing," I replied. "Why?"

"How would you like to come to our national sales meeting in Hawaii?" he replied.

"As what?" I tentatively asked.

"Our new sales rep!" he replied excitedly. "The company has never made an exception like this before, but since you have more experience than any candidate we've considered, you got the job."

I was stunned into silence.

truth. courage. *love.*

"Well? What do you think?"

"YES!" I blurted out happily. "Yes, I definitely want the job. Thank you!"

I loved being a pharmaceutical rep, except for the fact that it took me away from my family too often. But at the same time, I knew this job was the perfect opportunity that allowed me the security and independence I needed to support my family if Mark and I separated.

I went to counseling on my own for a while and finally, when I was about to walk out on our marriage, Mark agreed to go to counseling with me. We went for a good six months, but after a lot of trial and error, it became quite obvious that this marriage was not meant to be. The counseling was more about how to keep us together rather than addressing our problems as a couple. I was so disappointed, because I could tell things weren't going to get any better. I didn't want to break Mark's heart and devastate the boys. They loved their dad, and he was a great father. But ultimately, I told Mark, "I would like a trial separation."

That didn't set too well with him. "No," he replied. "If you want to leave this marriage in any way, then we are getting a divorce."

What? That seemed a little harsh. I thought he was testing me to see whether I would drop the whole thing if he drew a line in the sand. However, I knew that I would not be a good mother for my sons if I was dying inside, and not allowed to be the person I needed to be for them. If I couldn't be myself in this marriage, then I had no other choice but divorce.

"Fine," I replied. "Then I want a divorce."

He agreed a little too easily, probably because he didn't truly believe I would follow through with it. He did not want a divorce, but I knew in his heart that *he knew* that I had tried to make our marriage work. I never took our marriage lightly, and when I married him, I assumed it would be for life. But every relationship has its ups and downs, and since we had done everything we could to make it work, I was done trying.

Settling for Stability

Telling our sons was, to this day, the worst day of my life. They cried as if they were losing both of us. Alex was thirteen, and Connor was nine. We reassured them that they still had both of us forever, and that we both loved them very much. That part would never change.

After that, Mark moved out, and I moved forward with the divorce and mediation.

Even though it was what I really wanted, I couldn't believe that my marriage to my *stable, safe, and secure guy* was actually over.

truth. courage. *love*.

Terry at age fifteen in California with her sister Debi, Danny and grandparents Harry and Emma.

Terry at age thirty-four with her mom, and brothers Danny and John.

Terry Sidford

Terry at age thirty-four with her "big" little brother John.

Terry with her mom, and siblings Debi, Danny, and John on Danny's wedding day.

truth. courage. *love.*

Terry's mother in her high school photo.

Terry's mother in her thirties or forties.

Terry Sidford

Terry's mother in her sixties feeling happy and healthy.

Terry's dad at Palomar College working as a counselor.

truth. courage. *love.*

Terry's' father working as a counselor at a community college.

Terry and Matthew on their wedding day in 2005.

Terry Sidford

Terry and Matthew's 2005 wedding day with their combined four kids.

Terry at age fifty-eight in Park City, UT, living her best life!

truth. courage. *love.*

Terry at age fifty-eight living her best life.

Terry Sidford

Terry at age fifty-eight as a speaker, author, coach and thought leader.

Terry in Tuscany, Italy, celebrating her sixtieth birthday with her sons Alex and Connor.

truth. courage. love.

Terry celebrating her sixtieth birthday in Italy with her husband Matthew.

PART THREE

The Courage to Be Me
Chapter EIGHT

Acknowledging that Mark was not the right life partner for me was very hard to do. He was such a loving and wonderful father; logic dictated that I should love him. But Mark and I had two very different personality types, and I needed a husband that encouraged me to be my authentic self; someone who allowed me to grow, blossom, and fulfill my purpose in life, whatever that may be. I know Mark wanted to be that person. He really wanted to support me in my life dreams and make it work, but it wasn't fair to either one of us to keep trying when it was obvious that our marriage was not working. We had grown apart and evolved into people who wanted different things. I didn't want to waste his time nor mine going forward.

At this point, I was a forty-one-year-old, divorced, single mom who kept busy with work and family. I was okay with being single (possibly forever), because I knew that it was better to be by myself and feel whole than it was to be inauthentic just to be with someone else. And once I reconciled my relationship with my mother, I was finally at peace in a way I'd never been before.

On those few occasions when I did feel isolated or alone, I made a point of spending time with my friends. But after Mark and I parted ways, I quickly learned who my close friends were, as there were several who couldn't understand why I would leave such a good man and break up our family. Discovering that I had people in my life who couldn't be happy for Mark and me when we both decided to end an unhappy marriage was disappointing, to say the least.

truth. courage. *love.*

However, it was a painful lesson I had to learn. Whenever any relationship ends, there will always be people who just can't adapt to the new dynamic, and you have to be prepared to accept that.

Fortunately, my parents and siblings supported my decision to get a divorce, even though they were concerned about my future happiness and well-being. Honestly, the hardest part about ending my marriage with Mark was not being able to see my stepchildren as often as I had before. Although, I understand that their dad's happiness meant everything to them. They were protective and supportive of their father, so of course, when Mark and I split, they rallied around him. As they should have.

Looking back, I have the hindsight now to see that I divorced Mark when I was finally able to muster up the courage to say to myself, "Terry, if you want to keep growing, and move toward becoming the best possible version of yourself, then you can't stay married." I knew how Mark wanted me to be, and I would always feel guilty if I didn't act in a way that made him feel comfortable. I was outgoing, talkative, and a people pleaser. I needed lots of reassurance with more communication. Staying together would've not only been unfair to me but dishonest to him as well. It's unfortunate, but when two people grow apart and want different things, sometimes it's healthier to just admit they're not in sync anymore and part ways.

I know that's easier said than done, especially when you have a family to consider. I really had to dig deep to realize that my sons would be better off with a mother who was whole and fulfilled and living her purpose, rather than a shell of a person living a lie. Before Mark and I split up, I was not the best mother I could be because I was holding myself back and feeling resentful about it. I knew my heart had a lot more to give, but when you feel stuck, it's hard to see beyond today. My boys meant (and still mean) everything to me, so I wanted to be the best example I could possibly be for them. And watching their mother flounder in an unhappy marriage seemed criminal to me.

The Courage to Be Me

I watched my own mother slowly deteriorate in much the same way, and I wasn't about to do that to my own children. I just couldn't let history repeat itself.

Even though ending my marriage to Mark was the hardest thing to do, it was also the most courageous thing I'd done in my life since running away from my mother. But once I made that decision, and stood firm with it, I found that embracing my own strength during this time was empowering. It wasn't just leaving Mark that was so scary, but also knowing that I had to support myself and my boys, plus work full time. I had no idea how I was going to make all that work, but I had faith in myself to know that I *could* somehow make it happen.

And I did.

Somewhere deep inside me, I discovered a powerful, innate wisdom that helped me feel confident about making good decisions. My difficult life experiences had taught me invaluable life lessons that transformed me. For the first time, I began to evolve into someone I really liked. As I trusted this wisdom more, it got stronger and sharper, and a *new me* eventually emerged. As a result, I wanted to share my gifts and lessons with others, because I knew that if I could help other people find their own inner guiding voice, it could make a difference in their lives.

So once again, I went back to school and studied to become a life coach. I knew I had a gift to see people at the core of their heart. In time, I realized I had had this gift my entire life. I've always been able to see into people souls, into the center of their very being. I could feel who they were yet many times could not remember their names, because I only saw them from the *inside*. Instead, I remembered how they felt when I was around them. Growing up, I had this gift back then as well, but the adults in my life always explained it away by accusing me of being too sensitive. But I see now that it was just my highly-tuned intuition. And since no one could explain it to me, I just assumed something was wrong with me.

truth. courage. *love*.

Once Mark and I split up, all these emotional and insightful changes that came my way were scary, but I knew from my past experiences that I could handle just about anything. I was strong and resilient and trusted my knowingness. Because I let go of a lot of fear, I started to blossom and trust life. But most importantly, I trusted myself.

My inner changes affected my outer demeanor. Everyone saw a shift in me; I was happier and more confident. I said "yes" to everything in front of me. Life suddenly resonated as if it were a musical tuning fork. I was living my best life, and I did it on my own terms. I chose to find my happiness and life's purpose, and that purpose was to use my gifts and experience to make a difference in other people's lives. Coaching helped me hone my own purpose, and it showed me how my gifts supported my purpose. I felt so fulfilled helping others see their potential and live up to it.

I was also successful in my career as a pharmaceutical sales representative. It's funny because when I went to the sales trainings, I was always older than most of my colleagues who did the training with me, but I didn't care. In fact, I was very proud of my ability to learn everything I needed to know to do this job and be great at it.

Even though I was traveling as a pharmaceutical sales rep more than I would've liked, I was still able to settle into my new life as a single mom with the boys. I'm not going to lie, sometimes it was really hard to juggle everything. But regardless, up until then, I had never felt so free to be myself. The difference was that *this time* I wasn't just trying to survive like I had most of my life. Now I was living and thriving and choosing my own life's course. It was the best feeling in the world.

Although I wasn't looking to get into another relationship at that point, I started to date a little, just to test the waters. At that point, the bar for a boyfriend was so high, I wasn't sure if I'd ever get married again or even settle down with anyone. I had already decided that I would be fine living by myself the rest of my life.

And then I met someone in a coaching training. We were just friends and loved chatting before and after class. But it soon became apparent that he had other intentions. It had been eight months since Mark and I had split, and I hadn't seriously dated anyone up to this point, so I thought this guy might be a good reason to start dating again. He was nice and made for a good "rebound boyfriend," but nothing more. I knew this guy wasn't the person for me, but I figured it was time I got back on that wagon. Plus, I didn't see any harm in having fun.

The downside of this relationship was that he lived out of town, but eventually he got an opportunity to move to Salt Lake City for a job. When that time came, my kind nature got the best of me, and I offered to help him move. Once he got to town, his apartment wasn't quite ready yet. He asked if he could stay in my basement for a couple weeks until the apartment was ready. I didn't see any harm in that. But apparently, my ex-husband and everyone else around me thought it was an awful idea, because my sons were living with me, too. I didn't really care what others thought, but I also didn't want Mark to feel that our children were unsafe in their own home. Therefore, I decided to give this guy notice that he had a week to move out of my basement.

Of course, Basement Guy was not particularly happy about this, and who could blame him? He thought he had a place to stay indefinitely. But for me, my family came first.

Right around this time, one of my girlfriends asked if I wanted to go to a party. "But I have to warn you," she cautioned, "it will be all couples. You will most likely be the only single person there."

I was so frustrated with Basement Guy that I didn't care. "Yes," I immediately replied, excited for the distraction, "I would love to go!" I planned on leaving Basement Guy at home. Since it was a couples' party, I knew I'd be safe

truth. courage. *love.*

from meeting any potential dates. (I still wasn't sure if I even wanted to go out with anyone after dipping my toe back into the dating scene with Basement Guy.) Yes, I'd be the only single person at this party, but that also meant that I could just relax, have fun, and enjoy the evening.

The party was in an enormous, beautiful home that had a lot of unusual amenities, such as its own indoor basketball court. Regardless, the people were nice, the party mood was fun, and I put thoughts of Basement Guy on the back burner. Everything was perfect, and I was actually having a great time.

But then, a few hours into the evening, a man walked in the front door whom everyone seemed to know—especially the women—and they were all happy to see him. He was very handsome, with slightly long, blond hair. When he talked to people, he looked at each person as if they were the only one in the room. I was so amazed by his presence and charisma. As I watched him, I unintentionally analyzed him from head to toe with curiosity. He was different from everyone else, but I didn't know exactly how or why. Also, he was the only other single person there, which I didn't really notice until later.

As I chatted with other people, I suddenly heard a man's voice say, "Hi, I'm Matthew, who are you?"

I turned around and saw this same man five inches from my face. Startled, I backed away and said, "Terry. And what's your deal?" I couldn't believe I was so forward and cavalier in my response. That normally wasn't my nature. But in that moment, I felt I had nothing to lose by being honest. Besides, this guy had intrigued me. I wanted to hurry up and get past the small talk so I could get to know more about him.

Turns out he wanted the same thing. "No agenda," he said, "just saying hi." He smiled, and then I instantly knew why everyone felt so comfortable around him.

After that, we talked and hung out together the entire night. We made a real connection. Interestingly enough, it wasn't just me who noticed this.

The Courage to Be Me

Everyone around us saw that we were glued to each other the rest of the night. Eventually, we made our way to the basketball court to shoot some hoops. There was a moment while we were playing when he looked in my eyes and said, "Girl you've got game."

I smiled. I knew exactly what he meant, and it had nothing to do with basketball. He was seeing me as my best self, because I was comfortable in my own skin, being who I am. I allowed him to see this wonderful, fun, and funny person, whom I had previously hid from public view for so long. Honestly, in that moment, I felt seen for the first time, and it was magical.

At the end of the evening, he handed me his business card and I gave him my phone number. He hugged me and gave me a gentlemanly kiss on the cheek. I remember melting into his arms, lingering a little too long because I didn't want to let go. He released our embrace first, while I still awkwardly held on to him. Then I quickly let go when I realized I had this man in a death grip.

Upon arriving home, I told the Basement Guy, "You need to leave for good tomorrow."

"What? Why?" he asked concerned.

I decided to be honest with him. "I met someone tonight, and I don't want to blow it with him."

Basement Guy knew our relationship was just a fun thing for both of us and that it meant nothing in the long run. He could tell it was different with Matthew, and so he didn't try to persuade me otherwise. Instead, he just nodded without saying a word. The next day, Basement Guy moved out.

Also, the next morning, my friend who invited me to the party called and asked if Matthew had called me. At the same time, a friend of Matthew's called him to ask if he had called me yet. Apparently, our friends were eager for some phone calls to quickly take place.

As it turns out, Matthew *had* called me by then, and we'd set up our first date. I had no expectation, nor did I have any idea where this would lead.

Stepping into My Authentic Self
Chapter NINE

My life was finally on track, and I felt good about myself the night I went to the party and met Matthew. Even though it was a couples' party and I was going as a single, I went anyway to just mingle and have fun being around friends and new people.

But everything changed when Matthew came into my life.

When Matthew called me the next day to ask me on a date, I felt like a giddy teenager being invited to prom by the cutest boy at school. We had such a good time together at the party, I couldn't wait to learn more about him.

On our first date, he took me to dinner and we had deep, meaningful discussions during which we got to know each other better. He had a son, Royall, and a daughter, Lucy. I told him all about my two boys, Alex and Connor. He'd been divorced for two years, and my divorce had been final for well over a year. He was a successful realtor in Park City, Utah, and I had always wanted to live in Park City or go back to California.

Beyond having a lot in common, I found him to be refreshingly energetic and happy. His presence was positive, and his love for life was something I had not seen (at least to that magnitude) in anyone. Even though he'd been through his own divorce, he didn't harbor any bitterness of negativity about it. I could tell he had worked on himself, taking self-improvement courses to be the best he could in life, which impressed me. He was talking my language and I wanted more.

Stepping into My Authentic Self

I quickly realized that he checked all the boxes in terms of someone I could consider letting into my life. I found myself becoming even more enamored with this man before the night was over, and to my surprise, I had no reservations about getting serious with him.

After our first date, we became inseparable. It felt so refreshing to share myself with someone who didn't expect me to be anyone other than who I was. I didn't feel like I had to change to please him. I could totally be myself.

My only concern about our accelerated courtship was how my two sons felt about it. They were still young, and once Matthew and I started spending a lot of time together, Alex and Connor were not too excited about me getting serious with someone new. So I took it slowly.

I introduced the boys to Matthew not too long after we started dating. They thought he was nice, but I could tell they were keeping Matthew at a distance, especially Alex. Alex was thirteen, and he took the divorce hard. He was upset and challenged Matthew. However, Matthew never took anything the boys said or did personally. Instead, he held steady, not engaging in their pushback towards him, because he knew how important they were to me and our relationship. He saw the good in them, like he did everyone else, regardless of how they acted towards him.

It took some time, but eventually, we all started to feel comfortable together. A turning point came right before we got married, when we all went to Mexico on vacation. Matthew could always create magical moments in any situation, and he showcased this talent one night when he booked a dinner reservation for all four of us at a five-star hotel next door to our own hotel. It was the kind of place at which only Hollywood stars would visit, but somehow Matthew got us in. And my boys were so impressed!

During this unbelievable dinner, we sat outside and were treated like royalty. As the sun went down, the staff gave us ponchos to keep us warm and continued to spoil us with incredible food, all of which was backdropped against

truth. courage. *love.*

a gorgeous sunset and the sound of crashing waves. This relaxing atmosphere made the boys feel safe to open up and be themselves. As a result, the four of us engaged in deep conversations about how all our lives had changed so much in last few years and what it meant for the future. In that moment, I could tell that my sons' opinion of Matthew had shifted. I breathed easier knowing that it was the first step in creating a potential new family dynamic for all of us.

After dating for a year, Matthew and I both knew we had something magical. I was so happy with our relationship that I was fine with either continuing to just date or progressing to a "next step," whatever that may be. However, I'd learned my lesson from past mistakes, and I made it very clear that I would never move in with man unless we were married first (or at least had plans to be married in the very near future), especially since I had two sons to consider. From what I could tell, Matthew felt the same way. It was nice to be so in synch with someone when it came to those big, life decisions.

One of the many things that I love about Matthew is that he has good taste in food, wine, and travel. After we'd been dating for a while, he took me to dinner at La Calle, a fancy French restaurant in Salt Lake City. The dining experience there is exceptional. The beautiful grounds on which the restaurant sits are filled with roaming animals, bubbling streams, gorgeous flowers, and just about every outdoor natural feature you can think of—including occasional bad weather. While we were taking it all in, a storm rolled in and interrupted our dinner, which is not uncommon when you dine *al fresco* in the mountains.

As the rain started pounding down, I immediately wanted to run inside. Matthew, however, suggested we go sit on a bench out by the pond instead, where no one else was around. I thought he was crazy, but he gently insisted, so I went with it, just to be supportive. But once I was seated on the bench, he got down on one knee, took my hand, looked me in the eye lovingly, and said, "Terry, will you marry me?" Then he pulled out a stunning diamond ring.

Stepping into My Authentic Self

I was in shock. We had tentatively talked about a future together, but never anything definite by that point. I knew our relationship was on solid ground, but I didn't realize that he was ready to commit. For my part, I was already committed to him, and had been for a long time. Of course, I said, "Yes!" with all the love in my heart. I then threw my arms around him and gave him a big hug and kiss.

He proposed to me somewhere around the end of August or the beginning of September, and we were married on November 12, 2005, at a gorgeous ranch. It was that fast and everything I wanted it to be. My dear friend Laurie let me borrow her beautiful wedding dress. My sons were ages ten and fourteen, and by then, they had no trouble accepting Matthew as part of our family. They, along with a friend, played drums and guitar in a musical trio, providing a beautiful ambience to our wedding. Matthew's children, Lucy and Royall, were also there, along with Matthew's parents and a few of his closest friends. On my side, my father and his significant other, Sally, of course came, as did my mother and her husband, Bob. My brothers, Dan and John, and my sister, Debi, rounded out the rest of my family. They all showed up to support me and celebrate my happiness as I married the love of my life.

After the wedding, Matthew, my sons, and I moved into our new house in Park City. Then soon after that, I left my sixty-hour-a-week pharmaceutical sales job to work with Matthew in his real estate business. I got my real estate agent's license and we started selling homes and properties together. This new career path allowed me to have more flexibility in my schedule so I could stay home and take care of my boys, which I greatly appreciated. I no longer had to travel, go to an office, or work late. It was a blessing for me to be able to be there for my sons whenever they needed me.

Even though I gave up working in pharmaceuticals, I decided to continue my life coaching business, as it was something that fulfilled my soul. Helping other people has always been my purpose in life, but the pharmaceutical sales

truth. courage. *love*

job was how I was able to provide for my sons as a single mom. Now that I was working with Matthew, though, my schedule was dictated by my family and me.

Because our time was flexible, Matthew and I began to travel on fun adventures as my sons got older. We went all over the world, but wherever we were, Matthew was always attentive and considerate of me, making sure my needs were met in all aspects. This was something I was not accustomed to, but of course, I loved it! Honestly, I felt like I had to pinch myself sometimes, because after everything I had endured in life, I had to wonder if this was all real. *Did I really overcome a difficult childhood? Did I really find the courage to reconcile my relationship with my alcoholic mother? Did I really find the man of my dreams? Am I really living in one of the most beautiful places on the planet?*

My heart answered, "Yes, Terry, all those things happened. They led you here. This is real." From then on, I was filled with nothing but immense gratitude.

As I settled into the Park City community, I expanded the wellness aspect of my life coaching business by becoming a certified Pilates instructor and teaching at a local studio. I also started playing tennis at a local club. All of these new branches of my life allowed me to meet many wonderful new people, and to my amazement (and relief), I finally felt like I had found my tribe. I really fit in. As with Matthew, I didn't have to pretend to be another version of myself just to make everyone feel comfortable around me. Instead, everyone accepted me for who I was and loved me for it. They *got* me and didn't look at me as some troubled soul or an outsider trying to fit in. I can't put into words how *safe* that made me feel.

One morning, I was having coffee with my friend, Cindy, and she asked me how my coaching business was going.

I lit up like a lightbulb, because helping others was my favorite way to spend my time; it fed my soul. "You know," I said thoughtfully, "I've coached hundreds of people, mostly women, and there is one thing that doesn't make sense."

"What's that?" she asked.

"The majority of women I coach are incredibly resilient and courageous, but they don't see themselves that way. On the contrary, most of them see themselves as average, sometimes even as failures, even though they've accomplished truly unbelievable things against all odds."

"Wow, that's really interesting. I bet it would help these women, and others like them, if you could use their stories to make them see that they really are courageous. Have you ever thought about writing a book?"

I laughed at the thought. "I can't write a book. I don't even know *how* to write. I wouldn't know where to start."

"I'll help you," Cindy offered. "I really think this is something that needs to come out. You could start by doing a survey of women about how they perceive courage. Set a goal to gather surveys from one hundred women."

It was actually a great idea, but could I do it? I thought about it for a second. "Why not?" I finally said. "Let's give it a try."

It took a while, but I created the survey questions and eventually gathered exactly one hundred completed surveys from women of all walks of life. I was astounded by their answers and what they considered was courageous. All of them downplayed their own courage in one form or another. I knew I had to get this revelation out to the public.

A couple of local Park City writers helped me through the writing process, and I consider them my angels. They gave me the confidence I needed to collect these women's stories and document them in a book. It took a couple years to finish my book and, let me tell you, a lot of courage! Finally, after a lot of people's hard work, my book, *One Hundred Hearts: Inspiring Stories from the Women Who Lived Them*, was finally published, and it was one of the most thrilling days of my life.

After the book came out, I was at a book signing event when a lady in the audience asked me to give an example of my own courage.

"My own courage?" I was a bit taken aback.

"Yes. What's something you did in your life that was courageous?" she clarified.

I stood there dumbfounded. I had no idea what to say. *Had I ever been courageous?* It was in that moment that I realized I was just like the women in my survey. I could not recognize my own courage either. I really had to think hard about it, and still I came up with nothing.

That moment got me reflecting on my life stories, and over time, it led me to fully identify and embrace my own courage for the very first time in my life. It really took some soul searching to rewrite my story, to go from being ashamed of my life circumstances to seeing myself as a courageous woman, determined not to be victimized by my past and to change my life for the better. I began writing and talking about my transformation, and what led to it, with my friends and clients. Before long, my good friend, Rita, said, "Why don't you apply to speak at a TEDx event and tell your story of how you found your own courage?"

I appreciated her enthusiasm, but I knew better. "There is no way I will get accepted," I laughed. "I don't know how to formally speak in front of a large audience."

She shrugged, "What do you have to lose? Try anyway. I'll help you apply."

And she did.

Miraculously, the first application I put in accepted me, and four months later, I was onstage giving my TEDx speech, *Permission to Be Courageous*, at TEDx Twin Falls in Idaho (you can watch it on YouTube). In my talk, I told stories I had buried deep and kept hidden my entire life, but sharing these stories with an accepting audience was the most freeing and liberating moment of my life.

Stepping into My Authentic Self

My husband, sons, brother, sister, and many friends drove to Twin Falls to hear me speak. I felt so much love and admiration.

My biggest takeaway from all these experiences is that anything is possible *if you try*. If you don't try, nothing changes, right? At least if you try, and it doesn't work out, you're right where you started, which is the same place you'd be anyway if you hadn't tried.

But what if you try, and it *does* work out?

I wrote a book and did a TEDx talk when I had no experience or confidence that I could do either. But when I finally got onboard with the idea that I could do both, I said "YES" first and figured out how to make it work after. I pushed past my fears and achieved things I never thought possible. This led me to live outside of my comfort zone, leaning into the unknown for what was next, and even more so for what was possible. I started to *train* for my TEDx talk by enlisting to speak at local group meetings and professional organizations. I joined Toastmasters and got feedback from some of the best speakers in Utah. Before I knew it, I woke up one day and realized that I was living my dream as a motivational speaker.

Even though I'm not a trained writer, I found mentors who would read my writing and give me feedback. Then I looked for organizations that would appreciate my message, and as a result, I found places that would publish my writing. I became a contributing writer for an Australian health magazine called *The Great Health Guide*, and I have now been writing for them for over five years. I found that I have a talent and passion for writing that I never would have known had I not taken a risk on writing my book.

I have been a guest on hundreds of podcasts, and I started my own podcast called *The Choose Courage Movement*. As a result, I'm now considered a thought leader in regard to courage.

I continue to lean into life and all possibilities, living the *width* of my life, and not just the *length*. I wake up every morning feeling whole and complete. I always strive to be my best self in every moment of every day. I have no regrets, because I was courageous enough to confront the truth about my life and learn valuable lessons from it; lessons that allowed me to let go, become better, and share my resulting wisdom with my family and others. I found my passion and purpose, and I live life leading with abundant love, compassion, and kindness. I am complete, so everything from here on out is pure bonus. I have told my husband, sons, brothers, sister, mother, and father how much I love them and how much they mean to me. I have also shown them my truth and true self.

Now, at sixty years of age, I am exploring my spirituality in more depth. I never understood (nor completely aligned myself with) organized religion, yet I've always known that I was a spiritual being. The ability to see into others' souls was normal for me. People's names and how they looked on the outside never made sense to me. *I saw them from the inside.* I now know it's because I'm empathic. This explains my ups and downs emotionally throughout my life. I *know*, *feel* and *see* things deeply and differently from most people. I have loved deeply and hurt deeply. I can feel others' pain or love. I can walk into a room and feel the good, loving souls, as well as the negative, bad-intention souls. At meetings or events, I have actually changed seats to sit at another table, because I didn't feel good about the people already sitting there. And on the contrary, I've started conversations with people whom I've never met before but felt I'd known for lifetimes.

I do believe we have lived many lives and that our journey here is to learn lessons we have not yet learned completely. We must fulfill our purpose, use our gifts, and do our best to evolve beyond the limitations of our ego minds and physical bodies. We are much more than this existence. Love and compassion will teach us the lessons we need to learn. Love is our innate state of consciousness. It is *the* higher vibration that allows you to connect your higher consciousness to your innate wisdom and the knowledge you already have, as well

Stepping into My Authentic Self

as connect yourself with others. If you tap into this consciousness, you will find truths that cannot be explained in the physical form on this earth.

Pay attention to who you are and why you are here as you go along your life's journey. Learn lessons from your experiences and choices, good and bad. This perspective might make it easier for you to forgive yourself and others and return to love. All experiences are for our growth and evolution.

I learned a long time ago that forgiveness is the key to letting go of the past. You have to be happy in the present in order to create a positive future. Many people think forgiveness means accepting what others have done to you or what you have done to yourself. However, forgiveness doesn't mean making what happened right, that will never work, because you can't change the past. Instead, forgiveness is letting go of any negative energy associated with the past. Forgiveness will free you from the negativity brought on by the experiences that have been holding you back. Forgive and you will be free. And in return, love and joy will be in abundance. Your true self is a higher energy of love, joy, and happiness. I believe this is our authentic nature.

Find the truth of your life and allow yourself to be courageous enough to turn trials into triumph and pain into learning. If you want to improve your life, use the abundant love available to you to transform. Not only will you change, everyone else around you will too.

Today
Chapter TEN

The best thing about my life today is that I'm proud of the relationships I've cultivated, especially with my family members. As an adult looking back, I think people should be held accountable for their actions, but they shouldn't be shamed or defined by their mistakes for the rest of their lives. We are here to make mistakes and then learn and grow from them. None of us want to be held to the past forever, nor should we be. I realize now that everyone does their best, given the knowledge and experience they have to work with at the time.

And that includes my own family and me.

Whenever I share stories of my past, inevitably people want to know how everything turned out and where everyone is today. So, I thought I'd share an update on all the people in my story who matter to me most.

Mom

Although I have a good relationship with my mom today, it's bittersweet, because she suffers from dementia and has only short-term memory. However, she still knows her immediate family and lights up when any of us come to see her. She doesn't remember anything about her painful past. In some ways, that's a bit sad, because sprinkled among the pain, there were also some good times. But on the other hand, I have to say, without her long-term memory, she's the best version of herself now more than ever because she's not a victim of her past.

Today

I forgave my mom for her past behavior and the way she treated my siblings and me years ago. Today I love her unconditionally, and in return, I have received the kind, loving, funny mother I always knew she was deep down inside. Instead of blaming her for who she was, I try to make her feel safe to be herself today. We're at the point now that I've had many years of seeing my mom live entirely in the moment, which makes her much happier, and that makes me happy for her. I think we can all learn something from this ironic twist of fate.

Long before her memory loss, I asked my mom if I could be her power of attorney if there ever came a point at which she couldn't make decisions later in life. Well, that time has come, and I'm now one hundred percent responsible for my mother's care. Rather than looking at this as a burden, I'm honored to be in this position. Some people who know my family history have said to me, "It must be hard to be there for your mother when she wasn't there for you." My response to that is this; "Deep down, she's the same person I have always known. She had some struggles in life and overcame them. Now it's her turn to be taken care of, and she deserves it."

After getting reacquainted with my mom after I grew up, I can say with certainty that the last thing she ever wanted was to lose her children or hurt us. She was only trying to survive and do her best, according to what she understood at the time as a young wife and mother. Today, she deserves to know that she is loved unconditionally, regardless of the past that she doesn't remember anyway. I see the beautiful soul that she truly is, and I know that her family is everything to her.

Life has a way of coming around full circle. My life journey with my mother has taught me valuable lessons about forgiveness, unconditional love, courage, and compassion. She and I have been very close for many years. She knows I see her for who she is and that she is loved dearly.

truth. courage. *love.*

Dad

I have said repeatedly that my dad has nine lives, maybe even more! He is now eighty-seven and has survived many health challenges over the years, yet he still lives independently. I believe he keeps going because he loves life and his family. I talk with him almost every day, and he doesn't hesitate to tell me how proud he is of me and how much he loves and admires me. I have told him that despite the rough childhood my siblings and I endured (including living with him and his antics during the 1970s), he has always been consistent with his love for his kids. He still likes to talk about spirituality and life lessons, and he still leads with his heart, just as he has taught me how to do my entire life, even when I didn't always realize it.

The one thing about my dad that I have ALWAYS understood is his silly sense of humor. One of us will start cracking jokes, then we will bounce them off each other, and within a matter of seconds, we end up laughing so hard we both have tears streaming down our faces. What a tremendous gift to still have this interaction with my eighty-seven-year-old father. Through his love, sense of humor, and even his example, he has inspired me to go for it and live my dream to make a difference in people's lives as a coach, author, and speaker. As a teacher and counselor back in the day, he was, and always has always been, a seeker of truth. I'm thankful that he included me in his journey to find answers.

He and his live-in life partner, Sally, stayed together as a committed couple for almost thirty years, but they never married. However, they decided to go their separate ways around fifteen years ago. Today, Sally is happily married and lives in Carlsbad, California. Our family stays in touch with her, because she was a big part of our lives, especially when my siblings and I were growing up.

I'm grateful every day that I not only have my parents with me, but that I also get to experience the best of them both at this point in our lives.

Today

My Grandparents

I was lucky to have known both sets of my grandparents; my mother's parents and father's parents. Although, I have to say we were closer to my dad's parents, Emma and Harry Chittock. They were the grandparents with which we spent many childhood summers, and they were like my second parents.

My grandpa, Harry, was born and raised in Australia and was a professionally trained carpenter. He had the best sense of humor, a trait which my dad inherited. My grandma, Emma, was loving, emotional, and determined, but she had many health issues that inspired her to learn how to heal herself with natural remedies, which is how she came to eventually open The Cottage Health Food Store in Provo, Utah, long before health food stores were even a thing. I learned how to take care of my health because of my grandmother. We were very close, and I told her many times when I was young that she must have been my mother in a past life, and she agreed. She had difficulty conceiving and wanted many children but only had my father. Later, however, she adopted a young girl at age five and raised her as her own.

My grandfather continued working in construction well into his 70s, but when I was eighteen, he was hit by a car and killed at a job site. This was devasting to the family, and of course, particularly to our grandmother. She continued to live on her own for several years, and after I moved to Salt Lake City, I stayed in close contact with her. But unfortunately, it didn't take long before she developed Alzheimer's. As a result, she moved into a memory care facility, where she lived for many years until she passed in 1991 when I was pregnant with my son, Alex.

Orson and Bernice Tolman were my mother's parents; the ones my mother and I moved in with right after my parents split. After my mom and I moved back to Southern California, I didn't see these grandparents again until we went back to Utah for a summer visit. Unfortunately, my grandmother passed away in her fifties, when I was in seventh grade. This loss was particularly devastating for my mother because she was still in the depths of her alcoholism and couldn't go to the funeral. After my grandmother passed, my grandfather lived for many years and eventually remarried in is eighties. However, it wasn't too many years after that when he passed on as well. I will forever remember both my mom's parents as kind, loving grandparents.

Even though my grandparents sometimes didn't see eye to eye with my mom, especially after my mother left the Mormon church, Mom never said a bad word about her parents. They remained supportive and would've done anything for their daughter (and grandchildren). Today, my mom still remembers them and talks about them fondly. She has a photo of her parents next to her bed, and whenever we mention their names, she smiles and says, "I had such good parents." Mom always said she was lucky to have had such a loving family.

Debi

My sister, Debi, now lives in Oceanside, California, with her husband, Brett. They've been married for over twenty years now. Together they have seven children; six from Debi's previous marriage to her first husband, Cal (the one she married right after college), and one from Brett's previous marriage. Debi is a school teacher for a middle school in Carlsbad. She has two master's degrees and has been teaching for many years. We talk almost weekly and have a united commitment to caring for our aging parents. Debi loves—and is fiercely dedicated to—family. She will drop everything to be there for any one of us in an emergency. It's a quality in her that I deeply admire and respect, as she has repeatedly demonstrated her commitment to us during some of the most difficult times.

Danny

My brother, Danny, lives in Salt Lake with his wife, Lori, and they have two children. Danny has been a successful entrepreneur selling multi-level health products his entire life. He is a master at sales. He loves life and has a great sense of humor, just like my father. It is a rare occasion to ever see Danny unhappy or mad. He and Lori have huge hearts and would give a stranger the shirts off their backs. They are both incredibly giving, caring people. He loves our family, as well as his own, and is also dedicated to helping with our aging parents. I'm happy to say that he and I are still very close and we talk often.

John

My brother, John, is such a big teddy bear. I call him my big, little brother as he towers over me. He lives in Oceanside, California, and is on the front line with my sister caring for our mother. He has been a tattoo artist since he was around twenty years old, and as a gifted artist, he uses his talent for drawing in his career. He loves our family and feels grateful that he has Debi, Danny, and me as his siblings. We talk often, and he shares his humor and love abundantly.

Mark

My ex-husband, Mark, lives in Salt Lake City, Utah, and never remarried. He has continued to be a loving and stable father to our sons, Alex and Connor.

My Sons, Alex and Connor

Alex lives in Salt Lake City and has a successful career as a computer engineer and manager for a large company. He worked his way up from the bottom and is thriving at his job. He is a fiercely loving, sensitive, and adventurous person, and I couldn't be prouder of him as a son and individual.

Connor lives in Salt Lake City as well and also works as a computer engineer. He saw how Alex carved out a flexible career in which he could create his own schedule and work from home, thus allowing him the freedom to travel and be more in charge of his own time, so he followed in his older brother's footsteps. Connor is a sensitive, compassionate, loving son, and I'm just as proud of him for all he has become as I am of Alex for his accomplishments.

truth. courage. *love.*

I am lucky to have both my grown children live only thirty minutes away from me. As a result, we get to spend time together without having to travel great distances, which I truly appreciate.

Fortunately, my sons are close to Matthew and me as a couple. The four of us have traveled the world together, creating magical adventures wherever we go. I feel honored that they love to spend time with us, even though I'm a nerdy mom who would do anything to spend time with them.

That's it! Somehow, we've all survived life thus far, just as anyone does. Even if I could change any of it, I wouldn't, because my story has led me to where I am and who I am today. As a result, I'd like to leave you with a short list of wisdom that I encourage you to consider in your daily life. These are the encapsulated lessons I've learned on my journey.

1. The biggest "ah-ha" for me is that life, including close relationships, is a work in progress, every day and every moment of every year. Therefore, please NEVER give up on anything (or anyone) that matters to you, regardless of how impossible it may seem. If you have a dream, work one step at a time towards it. If you have a setback, learn something from it, get back up, and try again. Persistence is the key to getting what you want and being "who" you want to be, which leads to a happy, fulfilling, and successful life.

2. Don't be afraid to keep growing every day for the rest of your life. Strive to learn something new every day. We are all capable of greatness, and learning is the first step to getting there.

3. Make a difference in the lives of the people you encounter. If the only thing you do in a day is smile at a stranger, you've accomplished something incredible.

Today

4. Be the best person you're capable of being. Say "yes" and then figure it out. You will surprise yourself with what you can do.

5. Ask for help to achieve your goals. People want to help you succeed.

6. Create a tribe of people who lift you up and let go of people who drag you down. Life is meant to be filled with love, gratitude, giving, compassion, and joy. Don't waste a minute on negativity or activities that don't have meaning. Life is precious, and tomorrow is not promised to anyone. Live the width of your life, not just the length.

7. Be transparent and proud of who you are, regardless of all your bumps and bruises. Stay focused on the fact that you made it! It takes courage to let others see your true self, heart, and vulnerability, but it is worth it in the long run, because it's so much easier to just be who you are. And on the flip side, work hard to see others at their core, so they can also enjoy living an authentic life.

8. But above all, find your truth, courage, and love fully. Forgive and acknowledge the people you love, because once you do, I promise, anything's possible!

Afterthoughts
Chapter ELEVEN

I turned sixty years old this year. And although my book ends here, my story is far from over. I'm still growing and I'm still learning, and I plan to continue to do so for a very long time. But just from this little bit I've shared with you thus far, I can safely say that I've learned a lot. As a result, I want to share a few random afterthoughts of wisdom before we part ways. My learning curve on this journey has been immensely high, as I've clearly faced a variety of experiences, ranging from dealing with enormously fearful situations (starting at a very young age) to finding deep love both within myself and toward others. But in the end (or rather up to this point), the biggest "a-ha" for me is that I've learned it's always best to rely on your true self...even if the costs are high. Because the truth will never let you down.

Uncovering the truth about yourself (*your truth*), whether it's helpful or painful, allows you to see things for what they truly are. For example, when I was little, I was incredibly afraid of cliffs. When we drove on any road that was close to a cliff, I felt dizzy and nauseated. But as I grew up, I went hiking on and around cliffs, and the more I experienced them, the more I came to realize that looking down a cliff did not mean I would fall off the cliff. When I saw the truth about cliffs, my fear of them went away. I changed my truth from *cliffs are scary* to *cliffs won't hurt me, so they're not scary*.

When you find yourself stressed or anxious, it could be that you are not able to acknowledge the truth around what you feel or believe. Usually, this

Afterthoughts

means you're not honoring your own values or that you're not letting others (maybe even people you love) let you be who you are. In which case, it's time to uncover your truth.

Although uncovering your truth is a process, it's well worth the effort. When you let your authentic self be seen, it allows you to communicate with grace and confidence, and in turn people treat you with more respect. If they don't, then you didn't need those people in your life to begin with. There's nothing more powerful than uncovering your truth. The benefits are huge; there's less chance of miscommunication, it's easier and quicker to get to the point, and you'll always be clearly heard in the way in which you want to be heard.

To me, uncovering your truth is the very definition of courage.

And you know what? Courage is contagious. When we exhibit courage, other people follow suit. The easiest way to lead is by example because you're just being yourself. We all have so many opportunities to be courageous every day of our lives. Every time you take a stand for what is meaningful to you, you are being courageous. Never giving up is courageous. You will never regret trying your best, but you will always regret the opportunities you missed by not trying. If you stay clear and focused and don't compromise on the important things in life, you will be much happier and more fulfilled, and you will inspire others to do the same. You'll lift the people around you to stand up for their own values, prompting them to live happier lives, as well.

Although leading by example and leadership in general are common characteristics among both men and women, it's been my experience as a life coach that quite often women don't see the greatness in themselves. (In fact, my first book, *One Hundred Hearts: Inspiring Stories from the Women who Lived Them*, addresses that very issue.) If that sounds like you, then it's time to course correct. Focus on your passions and life's purpose instead of falling prey to all of the noise, fears, and naysayers in the world. Listen to your heart because when

truth. courage. *love*.

you're confident on your own path, that's when you can help others navigate their journeys. You don't have to have a big voice to do this. Sometimes, leadership is simply a quiet strength and resolve.

I know listening to your heart can be difficult, because sometimes what your heart tells you doesn't make sense at the time. But here's a little secret; your heart will never lie to you. It will always tell you the truth. The truth is consistent and never changes. You can rely on it. The truth is your inner wisdom, God, intuition, the universe, or whatever you believe to be your guiding spirit. The challenge is to know that your truth is always there. All you have to do is access it. Take the time to quiet your mind and be still, meditate, pray, or be in nature and *just listen*. You are fully capable of using your truth to find answers that will help you achieve your goals.

By tapping into my own truth, I've discovered something very powerful that has changed my life forever, which is this: *my story does not define me*. You read my story in the previous chapters, and you can plainly see that most of my past was not pleasant. In fact, a lot of it was downright painful. As a result, after I grew up, I mistakenly felt that I had no choice but to be a victim of my story and endure this victimization for the rest of my life. It was very convenient, because I could use my childhood story as a reason to not show up for myself or others. For example, I used it as an excuse as to why I never finished college, why my body wasn't perfect, why I allowed myself to get into bad relationships, why I didn't see myself as pretty; the list goes on.

But everything changed the day I realized that my perception of my past did not have to carry forward to my reality in the present (or into the future). When I let go of the story of my past and looked at it objectively, I knew the people in my past, particularly my mother, never wanted to hurt me in the first place. On the contrary, I could see that these people were actually hurting worse than I was. At that point, I knew from the depths of my soul that they needed my unconditional love and understanding, instead of my pity or

Afterthoughts

resentment. This shift revealed my own strength and allowed me to discover my true essence. Now I'm seen and heard for who I am (and for who I strive to be), and not for who I was in my old story.

Some people can't believe it when I say that I'm truly lucky to have experienced my past because it made me who I am today. Those people are usually the types that feel the need to control everything. Anything out of their control can cause anxiety and frustration. However, when you look at what you can and can't control by dividing the two, you will see the differences between them, which instantly brings you relief. For example, can you really control another person's actions? Can you control the weather? Can you control what the leaders of our county are doing? Not really. Sure, you can influence some of these things, but you cannot directly control *or change* any of them.

What you *can* control are your thoughts, beliefs, and actions toward various situations in life. When you start to feel out of control, challenge yourself to be mindful of how you *respond* to what's happening directly around you. You can choose what you say and do. No one can take those choices away from you. Look deep inside yourself to see what you're holding onto that you cannot control, and then let it go.

Many times, your need to control often results from fear; fear of the unknown, fear of failure, fear of change. Instead of running away from your fear, meet it head on by making an action plan to move past it. And with your new action plan in motion, you will soon find that the feeling of being out of control dissipates, until one day you notice it's gone. That's when you know you're at a turning point.

Like most people, I have experienced my share of trials, many of which I've shared with you in this book. But now that I'm on the other side of them, I see them as turning points in life. I didn't always look at them that way at the time they happened to me, but after a period of reflection, I could see that

truth. courage. love.

there was always something valuable to learn from these events. As a result, I initiated big changes in my life that may not have occurred otherwise.

I know it's hard to imagine, but you can almost always find opportunity in adversity. Once you push past your comfort zone, you will grow from the experience. Some of the most humbling and painful experiences in my life were the most transformative. We are here to grow from a life that gives us many challenges and even sometimes unimaginable pain. But how you handle these experiences is how you find out how resilient you are.

Why is it important to be resilient in the face of hardships and adversities? Because we're all faced with unknown challenges continuously throughout our lifetimes. You can't avoid them, but you can choose how to deal with these challenges and then thrive and grow as a result. Resilience is the ability to endure and bounce back from the difficulties you're forced to face.

I know sometimes this is easier said than done. Your thoughts are powerful, and when you go down a path of overthinking or "what-ifs," then those thoughts are not always helpful or even accurate. When this happens, it can be easy to fall into fear-based thinking, which can paralyze you from taking productive action—or even any action at all.

To get unstuck, I like to change my perspective of fear. To do this, I look at the word FEAR as the acronym, *Face Everything and Rise*. Because when you consider the things that you're most afraid of, you realize the majority of what you fear *never actually happens*. Or at least it doesn't happen to the degree you feared. Instead of backing down from fear, keep going and push through it. You might surprise yourself and come out on the other side with a gift you never thought possible.

And one of those possible gifts is love.

Although *love* comes in many forms (romantic, friendships, strangers, pets, children, food, nature, hobbies, etc.), self-love is the hardest one to achieve, yet it's the one we need the most. Self-love is connecting to that same

Afterthoughts

feeling of acceptance with affection and admiration that you would give to someone else. Why is it so hard for us to love ourselves? In my journey, I've discovered that knowing love within yourself allows you to express it with others (and in life) more fully. I also believe that the feeling of love is our natural condition. It's our highest vibrational state and connects all of us on a spiritual level. That said, one of my favorite quotes is by Adrienne Maree Brown when she said, "Love allows us to flow together toward a shared future."

People generally believe that the opposite of love is hate. But really, the opposite of love is *fear*. We are either experiencing love or fear. It is impossible to feel these two emotions at the same time. So, you are in either one state or the other. When you experience fear, you block out the love of yourself and others. Your true judgment is hindered, and as a result, you struggle to trust or make good decisions.

But when you feel love, you are more grounded and connected to your true nature and best self. Being in a state of love is when you're able to uncover your truth and make good decisions. You will also be able to see the love in others and in life in general.

Lucky for us, love is the universal solvent of most problems. Because it runs at a higher frequency of energy, it allows you to operate at your ideal human and spiritual level. You attract similar energy fields around you, so choosing to love and be loved helps you gracefully get around obstacles and overcome challenges.

That's not to say that fear doesn't have its place. Fear is a natural part of life, but if you are aware of it, then you can greet it with loving eyes and then choose to love instead. We always have a choice in every moment to choose love and courage over fear and doubt. In one of its earliest forms, the word courage meant "To speak one's mind by telling all one's heart." Therefore, choosing love is a form of courage.

truth. courage. *love.*

HeartMath has done many studies on the connection between your heart and brain. The heart regulates the brain and coherent (or incoherent) frequencies in your body, and then in turn, it regulates your *happy* or *stress* hormones. It's a scientific fact that your feelings and thoughts impact your physical body. It's interesting to also note that the heart frequency can be measured up to three feet away from the body, but the brain is measured only about one foot from the body. This means that the frequency of love that comes from your heart emanates to others much further around you than the energy that comes from your brain. For example, think of a time you met a stranger and felt their kindness or love instantly. Or when you saw someone from across a room and you knew instantly that they were a good person, and so you went over to talk to them. Or think of love at first sight. How many stories have we heard of people that knew the moment they met that they would fall in love and be together forever? And then they did and were.

Knowing this, it's important to take time every day to be aware of your feelings and ask yourself, "Am I choosing love over negative thoughts of fear and doubt?" Listen for the answer and then course correct to steer yourself toward positive or loving feelings. Because when you do, you will see everything and everyone around you transform to be aligned with the life you want and deserve.

It worked for me. And it can work for you.

Acknowledgments

First and foremost, I'd like to thank my parents, starting with my sweet mother, Laure June Elsasser, who taught me to be kind, loving, and courageous. I love you to the moon and back, Mom. Also a big thanks to my father, David Harry Chittock, who taught me to laugh, love, and be the best version of myself, no matter how difficult life may get. You inspired me to understand my spirituality and you always believed in me.

My deepest heartfelt thanks to my brothers, who are always looking out for me. I appreciate that you love fiercely and make me laugh and feel loved. I love you both more than you know.

To my wise sister, who protected me, taught me to be brave, and to never give up. Your example of overcoming adversity while staying strong has been a constant inspiration in my life. I love you very much.

To my amazing husband, Matthew, thank you for telling me every day how beautiful I am, regardless of how I look. I love that you love me unconditionally. Thank you for all your support in following my dreams and being my best self. My life has been an incredible adventure with you. I love you always!!

To my son Alex, you light me up and make me whole. Your constant love, support, and humor fill my soul, and your hugs melt my heart. I love you always and forever.

truth. courage. *love.*

To my son Connor, you are a special one. You are constantly observing and know what I need. Your love is priceless and fills me up inside. Your hugs melt me, too. Love you always and forever.

Many thanks to my editor, Stacy Dymalski, for helping me on this journey of writing this book. Your encouragement, love, and belief in my life story has helped me stay inspired and kept me going. You have cheered me on the entire way to get this book finished by my sixtieth birthday month, and for that I am so grateful.

A special thank you to my lifelong friend from high school, Stacey Clavier, who has been by my side to help edit all my writing materials.

Thank you to the *Great Health Guide* for continuing to support my writing and publishing my articles.

To all my friends who have seen me, supported me, and been there through the best and worst times. Thank you. You are all the best!

To all the spiritual leaders in the world, past and present. Thank you for shining your wisdom and light and showing us the way.

Thank you to the people whom I had to dig deep to forgive. You taught me how to be courageous and continue to shine in my life after adversity.

And finally, thank you to all the people who have inspired me to be courageous and share my story. I hope the people who read my story can gain some insight that is helpful in their own lives.

About the Author

Terry is a sought-after motivational TEDx speaker, Author, Life Coach since 1998, and host of the Choose Courage Podcast. She has assisted scores of people and organizations in achieving their dreams, which she believes is her own life's purpose. Terry's greatest joy has always been to help others unleash their potential and live life to the fullest.

Based on her success as a professional coach and thought leader, in her research on the benefits of owning your courage, she has been asked to speak at many personal growth and business-related events.

Terry has spent over half her life acquiring the knowledge and experience that qualify her to guide others. The acquisition of those experiences is the basis for her book *One Hundred Hearts: Inspiring Stories from the Women Who Lived Them*, a collection of stories of female courage in the face of adversity.

truth. courage. *love*.

Terry is also a certified Passion Test facilitator, accredited Pilates instructor, author of two books and a popular newsletter that showcases her personal experiences and insights, as well as a regular contributor to a national wellness magazine, "The Great Health Guide."

Terry was raised in Southern California and has lived in Utah for more than thirty years. She's active in the outdoors, plays tennis, runs, and skis. Currently she resides in Park City with her husband, Matthew, and has two sons, Alex and Connor, and two step children Royall and Lucy.

www.ingramcontent.com/pod-product-compliance
Lightning Source LLC
Chambersburg PA
CBHW072037110526
44592CB00012B/1457